THE 30-MINUTE GARDENER

THE
30-Minute
Gardener

Cultivate Beauty and Joy
by Gardening Every Day

Greg Loades

With photography by Neil Hepworth

Timber Press
Portland, Oregon

Published in 2023 by Timber Press, Inc., a subsidiary of Workman
Publishing Co., Inc., a subsidiary of Hachette Book Group, Inc.
1290 Avenue of the Americas New York, New York 10104
timberpress.com

Printed in China on paper from responsible sources
Text and cover design by Vincent James

The Hachette Speakers Bureau provides a wide range of authors for
speaking events. To find out more, go to hachettespeakersbureau.
com or email HachetteSpeakers@hbgusa.com.

ISBN 978-1-64326-133-1

Catalog records for this book are available from the Library of
Congress and the British Library.

To Zachary,
the man with the watering can

Contents

Preface

It's two weeks until Christmas and the geese are flying home. I know because I can hear them calling, like a warning bell that winter is here. The grey clouds are looming ominously in the east and the sun is long gone to the west. It's half past four in the afternoon and everyone's leaving. Except me. Here I am with a digging fork in my hand, beaten-up old trainers on my feet, and a line of brambles in front of me.

What am I doing out here? Why haven't I headed for the couch, with the central heating and the tv streaming service at the ready? Isn't it too cold to be messing about outdoors?

More often than not, you will find me out in the garden.

Well, no, because out here, alone in the fading light, is where I belong and where I feel most alive.

My journey started a long time ago, or so it feels, when I was a small boy. I grew up on a farm and got involved from a young age. By the time I was eleven, I would spend summer holidays planting fields with Brussels sprouts and cabbages for winter harvest, or pulling out weeds that I swear were taller than I was (perhaps I was very small or these were good years for the weeds). In any case, ever since then I've spent as much time outdoors as possible.

An understanding of the changing seasons came naturally to me, as did a sense of how they relate to being a gardener. I haven't always had a lot of growing space available, but this feeling has never left me: that gardening gives me a chance to connect with nature, to live life at a slower pace, and to gain perspective on the things that compete for my time and attention.

Maybe you feel this way too. Making a garden, savouring a garden, living and breathing a garden, comes from a spark inside of us that once lit will not be put out. So how does this relationship begin, and is it possible anywhere?

Whatever growing space you have, connecting to it every day can ignite a process that will enrich your life. Maybe for you the garden is a few pots on a balcony or windowsill, or perhaps it's an area that seems big and untamable. Half an hour a day is enough time to become attached to a natural world, and this relationship will help you put problems into fresh context, not to mention inspire you (or me) to create a new garden.

The journey to becoming a 30-minutes-a-day gardener starts here. And if you choose to take it, you may never see life the same way again.

Being in the garden

An introduction

Dare to discover another life
Walk along well-trodden paths
Find joy in unexpected places

Rosa 'Felicia' with
Hebe 'Silver Queen'
and *Carex oshimensis*
'Everillo'

W̲e can find ourselves in gardens for so many reasons. Perhaps we need somewhere to hang out the
laundry, or to give children some fresh air because
they are driving us crazy indoors. Maybe the reason to spend
time in the garden is to catch up on a good book on a sunny
day off work, or to host a picnic on the lawn for family and
friends. None of these things involves having green fingers
or a green thumb, perhaps just a working knowledge of a
lawnmower. All this may seem rather obvious, but the point
is that gardens can be largely ignored even when they are still
used, with the user oblivious to the possibilities that await
if nurturing the garden and being in the garden become a
year-round, daily habit.

Alternatively, gardens can easily end up as utility spaces,
infrequently visited and even then only for life's mundane routines or occasional social appointments. The calendar tells you
that a friend is coming to visit tomorrow. The weather is warm
and sunny, summer is in full swing, and a glance at the garden
creates that feeling of dread. It's scruffy and overgrown and
the only way to get it ready for your friend is to give it a blitz.
Maybe you're familiar with the process. Out come all the tools
for hacking and slashing. For a few hours in the summer heat,
grass and weeds are flying amid a frenzy of noise, perspiration,
and the awakening of previously dormant muscles from their
sleep. Burgeoning plants are resented: those that looked neat
a few years ago have now muscled into the patio space and
cast unwanted shade.

I have a similar relationship with household chores. I don't
notice that they need doing until the results of my inactivity
become impossible to ignore—the stack of plates to wash, the

piles of laundry that need attending to, or the rug that needs a good vacuum.

We can't hide from the fact that like homes, gardens need attention. And they need time. But unlike the inanimate objects that household chores are made up of—and it's amazing how much I can loathe a saucepan when it has yesterday's porridge stuck to it—a garden is a living, breathing abundance of life in all its diversity. Engage with it daily, nurture it, and you will discover something more deeply rewarding than the feeling of having a clean house or a wardrobe of fresh clothes.

As we turn our attention to our outdoor space on a regular basis, we find an escape from the madness of modern life. An opportunity opens to be part of what it has meant to be human for millennia: growing plants and tending a place on the earth. Focus on the garden and in turn our world starts to realign. Regularly spending time in the garden encourages us to notice small things, such as seeds or new shoots which can easily go unnoticed, and to watch their slow development with wonder—the antithesis of a world where instant gratification has become the norm.

Our goal in becoming 30-minutes-a-day gardeners is not to make an efficient garden-maintenance regime (sounds too much like doing the dishes to me), but rather to open the door to a parallel universe that is bursting with life, to delight in the process of natural growth, and to embrace nature's pace.

Oh, and once you are in the 30-minutes-a-day habit, you will probably notice that your garden isn't out of control. And you'll come to agree that this is a byproduct of a new way of life rather than the purpose of it.

Discovering the cycle of life

Embracing nature's pace

If our relationship with our gardens is one of detachment, then it is easy to resent growth. The lawn is too long. That climbing plant by the back door is out of control. Those weeds in the cracks in the patio are taking over. In contrast, as with any relationship, this one is far more likely to blossom if we find quality time for it. As we start to venture out into the garden for 30 minutes a day, hear the birdsong or the background hum of pollinating insects, take some deep breaths, observe the changes, and pay more attention to nature. This is when an understanding begins. We are all just doing our best to live, whether we are humans, grasses, insects, or weeds. Your garden is an orchestra playing a symphony, and you get the privilege of being at various times the conductor and the audience, sometimes coaxing the best from a natural talent, at other times reining in youthful exuberance, and at the best times, simply basking in the glory of the music.

The development of a garden is like the sound of a song that can't be silenced. A haze of green shoots emerging in a tree or hedgerow is a powerful force, a constant in an ever-changing world. Perhaps now more than ever, a garden can be a place of comfort, not just for our physical well-being but for our mental and spiritual existence too. Step out into the garden and wherever you look, there will be a reminder of the cycle of life: a worm just beneath the soil surface, discovered as you dig with your trowel (or in my case, discovered by my son and adopted as a pet for the rest of the afternoon), or perhaps some dandelions flowering in the cracks in an old wall (a nuisance weed or a source of free salad, depending on how you look at it).

There is so much to discover in our gardens and if we decide that being there matters as much as the day job, the gym class, or the streaming options, then we will begin a

Witnessing the burst of new growth from something that was once bare is among the wonders of gardening.

journey that not only puts our lives into context, but also changes them for the better. We may have made that journey to the bottom of the garden a thousand times to collect the washing or to put some unwanted household junk into the shed. Or maybe it's the world of work that swallows up so much of our time and thinking. Like metal detectorists discovering gold, we can also unearth unknown treasure that was there all along. We just have to take the time to stop, press pause, and discover it.

Do you struggle to escape from a need for instant gratification? If so, you're in good company. I love numbers, and in this era of social media, life can be consumed by wanting to know how many followers you have. I have two minutes to spare—let's see if anyone else liked that post that I checked five minutes ago. Or how many minutes of screen time have I had today compared to yesterday? Have I managed to shave off a few minutes? Am I winning or losing? It seems that we record more and more of our day, from the length of our sleep patterns to the numbers of steps we've taken, as if the quality of our lives can be scaled down to good or bad statistics.

You can see why I am so grateful to be spending regular time in the garden. I have no apps telling me how long germination has been for a particular crop, how many flowers have appeared compared to last year, or how many blueberries I harvested compared to the previous summer. But more importantly, I have no choice but to take life at nature's pace. And nature offers no promise of instant gratification. Unless you get the keys to a garden, walk in, and find a bed of strawberry plants bearing perfectly ripe fruits (I'm sure I had a dream like that one time), then to garden is to live by the adage that good things come to those who wait.

At a time when television programmes are criticized because only one new episode is made available per week, it is nothing less than countercultural to embark on a hobby that asks you to wait weeks, months, or even years for the next episode. And why would anyone do such a thing? We garden because doing so offers us the privilege of working with nature to see something beautiful come to life. And surely nothing tastes as sweet as a strawberry that you've grown yourself through to delicious ripeness.

Shifting our focus

How do you become a 30-minutes-a-day gardener?

This question brings to mind some advice given to me by the much-loved British gardener, broadcaster, and plant explorer Roy Lancaster. He told me that to embark on a career in horticulture required three things: patience, adventure, and curiosity. For me, this perfectly sums up how to embrace and enjoy the benefits of life in a garden. It doesn't sound like much—over the years I've used the acronym PAC to make sure that I remember it—but I believe it is the essence of what we need in order to get into the 30-minutes-a-day habit.

A sense of adventure has helped me practice patience as a gardener and it has also inspired me to experiment with plants. I've found through experience that I am far more likely to wait patiently for results if I set in motion a project that I really believe in and have orchestrated myself. My north-facing front garden is a prime example. There are plenty of plants labelled as shade-lovers that I could have decided to grow in this garden, and I have grown some of them. But I have also experimented by planting some plants that aren't famed for their tolerance of shade, and then I am excited to see what happens with another one of my crazy ideas. This adventurousness goes hand in hand with curiosity.

It is also easier to be patient, adventurous, and curious if we concentrate on growing what we want to grow. This might sound obvious, but it is so easy to fall into the trap of just growing what you see by accident in the plant centre rather than seeking out something that appeals to you more. Or maybe we grow something because grandma used to grow it. Or because a friend gave us a plant that, truth be told, we don't really like but couldn't refuse (hands up with me if you're not good at saying no to a gift). This is why some gardeners give up: why grow plants that you don't love?

To see something through, we also have to really want results. Otherwise, it's a bit like being persuaded by a friend to go to a vegan restaurant when you really feel like eating fried chicken. Your heart won't be in it. Grow vegetables that you think are delicious. Grow flowers that you think are truly beautiful. Then patience, adventure, and curiosity will all roll into one.

Facing north

A calm place in the garden

My north-facing front garden also means something else to me. Most of the plants here rarely see the sun, even on a cloudless day. It can be a hot, sun-drenched afternoon just a few steps away in the south-facing back garden, with plenty of plants to water and hot faces to smother in sunscreen, but in the front garden it is cool, calm, and peaceful. In truth, it is a far more relaxing space in the height of summer than the sunbaked back-yard that British gardeners tend to flock to, probably because they don't know when they will experience hot sun again.

Yet we all need a place where we can cool off from the searing heat of life—to escape from the strained relationships, money worries, workplace drama—and to sit for those precious minutes, reflect, tend to our plants, harvest crops, and take pleasure in the scene. Once we are in the habit, venturing into our garden, regardless of its geographical orientation, is like

choosing to be somewhere that faces north at the end of a tiring day, and as we do, the sun isn't quite so wearing. Developing the 30-minutes-a-day habit is like standing up to a playground bully. The bully's heat begins to fade. We may be "facing

My north-facing front garden is a place of calm and coolness in the height of summer.

north" only metaphorically, but the garden, balcony, or growing space offers true perspective and peace.

In fact, to get the most from this book, I strongly recommend devoting at least one 30-minute stint a week to facing north, just sitting in the garden (facing in any direction) or walking around and taking it all in. At the end, write down everything that you observe: progress, wildlife, weather, new flowers or fruits, successes, and failures. This will create an essential account of the year to look back on, to serve as a reminder of the fundamental, ever-changing dynamic of a garden and to remind you of the wonder of this world-within-a-world that once embraced is not readily discarded.

As we spend more time in the garden, we develop a healthy habit that provides an escape from the madness of the world and rediscover nothing short of what it means to be alive. I hope you will join me on the adventure of a lifetime. Maybe this all sounds too good to be true, but here it is. Whatever the season, whatever the space, and whatever your garden looks like right now, this is a perfect time to begin.

1

Belonging in the garden

Begin with a few simple steps

Now there's a chance to recharge and unwind
Escape all the screens and the ongoing grind
Leave all the stress and the madness behind
I belong in the garden

The view from my
comfortable place by
the back door in my
previous backyard
garden.

C arving out 30 minutes a day to spend in the garden might be a challenge for you at first, especially if it's winter and dark for much of the day. But it is amazing how quickly half an hour disappears when you get involved in something you enjoy. Think how quickly 30 minutes vanishes into thin air when you are watching a favourite tv show or listening to a much-loved collection of songs. If you are new to the process of getting out in the garden to grow things rather than doing chores, then the habit may take a while to kick in, a bit like that habit to go running every day that I have tried to set in motion for at least the last decade (I'm still trying with that one).

For me, though, finding that precious half hour for the garden is not an appointment in my diary or a reminder on my phone but something more opportunistic. It could be early in the morning if the kids have decided to sleep in and let me make a peaceful coffee, a rare event but it does happen occasionally. Or it might be a lunch break when I'm home working and need to take my eyes off the screen or playtime with my toddler when he needs some fresh air—you get the gist. When spending 30 minutes in the garden becomes part of your way of life, it isn't a planned event: it weaves its way through all the busyness of work, play, family, friends, and all the things that make life what it is.

Maybe you're thinking, well that's nice and fine for you once you're in the habit, but where do I begin? And that's a great thought to have. To take the running analogy again, is there anything worse than listening to that smug colleague at a 9 a.m. work meeting who tells you that they've come back from a quick 10k, made waffles and a fresh pot of coffee, and were still on the call five minutes early while they waited for all the mere mortals to scrape there on time?

Let's look at how to get in the habit of being in the garden every day and all the benefits it brings.

It can take a while for gardening to become part of life if you're starting from scratch or if you have become disconnected by the time-consuming duties of life. I've been there myself. For a while I had a long commute to London every day to work, and then later on I lived and worked in the city. My connection to the changing seasons and the natural world was still there, but it had become dulled by hours spent on cramped trains, lack of growing space, and that dizzy feeling of having been churned up by the rat race.

Yet this was when I most needed a respite from the crowds, the concrete, and the congestion. The hedgerows, wildflowers, and fresh vegetables of my youth were a distant memory rather than a daily pleasure. It was then that I realized that the 30-minutes-a-day-in-the-garden habit that had been a subconscious fixture in my life would now need to be worked at more. The process of growing things was not only countercultural, it was critical to finding an escape from the grind. And fortunately I remembered that a simple seed could transform a life.

An acorn or a tiny seed

Dream big because the sky's the limit

I can think of no better way to begin the journey to being a
30-minutes-a-day gardener than by sowing some seeds. No
matter which seeds you choose to sow, or how long it takes to
germinate and become something beautiful, you are embark-
ing on gardening's greatest miracle. I still get excited when
seeds start to sprout. That moment when the compost bulges
and you catch a glimpse of a stem starting to unfurl is both a
story with a happy ending and the thrill of a new beginning.
You have sown a seed that germinated. New life has begun,
whether in your allotment or community garden space, your
own backyard or large garden, or on your windowsill. Whatever the context, whatever the plant, something has grown
from nothing. And that's something to get excited about,
whether it's for the first or the fiftieth time.

Thus begins the habit of daily checking, which for me is the
natural world equivalent of scanning a cell phone for Facebook
likes. I probably check pots of sown seeds at least three times a
day, often knowing that it is far too early for anything to happen.
Or if you put your pots or trays of seeds on the kitchen windowsill, you will be forever keeping an eye on them (unless you take
my approach to washing plates).

If you're not a confident seed-sower, start with large seeds,
which tend to be easier to handle and sow. I love the thick, curly
seeds of pot marigolds (*Calendula officinalis*), which resemble
an ultra-miniature form of a children's snack. If you think I'm
crazy, imagine them four times as big and covered in salt or
syrup. I sprinkle them everywhere in early spring: along the
edges of paths and in gaps in the border where I know that
some hot orange flowers will be most welcome in the second
half of summer. There's no need to wait for warm weather to
sow these amazing seeds: pot marigolds are considered hardy

Pot marigolds (*Calen-
dula officinalis*) are
easy summer flowers
to grow from seed.

HARDINESS RATINGS

A plant's hardiness zone rating is generally based on the minimum temperatures at which it will survive. The hardiness zone doesn't reflect other requirements that plants have, for example, for light and moisture. And zone ratings don't take a garden's microclimates or a gardener's judgment into account. As the USDA says, "No hardiness zone map can take the place of the detailed knowledge that gardeners pick up about their own gardens through hands-on experience."

U.S. Department of Agriculture hardiness zones are based on average annual minimum temperatures over a 30-year period. The lower the zone number, the colder the winter temperatures. Including a range of zones is meant to suggest the maximum as well as the minimum temperatures at which the plant will survive.

To see temperature equivalents for each USDA zone and to learn in which one you garden, see the interactive USDA Plant Hardiness Zone Map at planthardiness.ars.usda.gov/

The Royal Horticultural Society's hardiness ratings for garden plants are based on "absolute minimum winter temperatures (°C), not the long-term average annual extreme minimum temperature used for the USDA zones." Download the table from rhs.org.uk/plants/pdfs/2012_rhs-hardiness-rating.pdf.

For Canada, go to planthardiness.gc.ca/.

For Europe, go to uk.gardenweb.com/forums/zones/hze.html.

Pencil it in

Before transplanting seedlings
from their trays, use a pencil to
make a deep hole in the centre
of the compost in each new pot.
Then the seedlings can be easily
dropped into the new pots without the roots being squashed.

annuals, rated as hardy to UK zone 6 and
in USDA zones 2a to 11b.

The experts probably wouldn't recommend transplanting them, but I also
start some pot marigolds in trays in the
kitchen, scattering the seeds lightly on
the compost surface and covering them.
Then I use my trusty pencil to tease out
the tiny plants to grow in individual
5cm (2in) pots, and I keep potting them
up as the roots continue to fill the pots.

Gently tip a pot or two upside down to have a look. This is
a job that teaches patience because if you start tipping them
upside down every day to check, it's easy to have an accident
with the ones that haven't rooted yet and find yourself with
a small heap of compost and a squashed seedling. I've done
this plenty of times in my eagerness to get things done in the
garden in spring. Best not to beat yourself up though, because
as I try to remind myself all the time, gardening shouldn't be
a competition. There are no winners or losers. If we decide
to engage with the world of growing plants, with its inherent
beauty, we are all winners.

Once the plants are sturdy, I plant them out, throwing a
handful of compost into the hole first, and they keep flowering
until frost (or fall mildew) finishes them off. If your soil is light
and sandy, then you may well see the seedlings popping up in
the following year unaided, more of nature's wonder to behold
in early spring. You'll most probably stumble across them on
that morning walk through the garden. That's the beauty of
what we're doing.

Sowing seeds and teasing out seedlings into their own space
so that they can begin life on their own in the big wide world
presents an obvious parallel with raising children or pets. You've
begun the process of nurturing a living thing, which in turn

SEED-SOWING SUCCESS

If you are not sure how deep to sow seeds, a good rule of thumb is to cover them with a layer of sieved compost or vermiculite that is twice as deep as the height of a seed.

Try to space out the seeds evenly and avoid sowing them in big piles. Spacing the seeds will make the seedlings much easier to transplant later.

If the compost goes dusty and dry, water pots and trays from the bottom by placing them in trays of room-temperature water.

needs regular attention, although thankfully you don't have to worry about youngster plants writing on the walls or digging up the lawn.

And the same goes if you start your habit by buying some young plants. This definitely isn't cheating. There are no medals awarded for growing from seed (okay, maybe in some areas of competitive horticulture but that's, in truth, another world). The process is the same. Once we get in the 30-minutes-a-day habit, you have a living thing that you will make a connection with as it grows. And grows. In fact, I should offer some words of encouragement to anyone who would refer to their garden as a jungle and not in a good sense.

Clearing an overgrown garden

Just take it step by step

Remember that garden full of ripe strawberries that I dreamed about earlier? Well, you can keep it! There is something incredibly rewarding and satisfying about overhauling an unkempt garden. Can it be done in 30 minutes a day? Definitely. In fact, if you are faced with an overgrown jungle, I would say that you are in a perfect position to get the 30-minutes-a-day bug.

I've had my fair share of wilderness gardens. My home garden when we moved in is a prime example: an intimidating thing with endless thickets of menacing, skin-scraping, splinter-inducing brambles; soul-destroying clumps of thick, tufty grass that could host an all-you-can-eat buffet for a herd of sheep and still look overgrown at the end; and thistles that had seeded themselves from the top of the garden to the bottom. And to make matters worse, it was growing atop a 10cm (4in) layer of stones. Anyone who came to visit

My garden, when I first got the keys to the house, was over-grown to say the least

our house when we moved in would take one look at the garden and say "You've got your work cut out" or "Good luck."

My response was always the same: "It's not a problem. It'll be fine." No one seemed to believe me. In fact, most people looked at me like I was from another planet. You'll get this once you're in the gardening habit. It doesn't make sense to everyone. Fair enough—everyone's entitled to their opinion. But stick to your guns and don't be put off by a wilderness. I'll tell you why.

Tackle it bit by bit and you'll realize that you have the chance to work with nature to make that relaxing space that you always wanted. Where to start is less important than how to start. In my garden there were yards and yards of weeds to remove, but I did it literally 30 minutes a day. I had no choice but to have a limit. It was winter, work was piling up indoors (along with the dirty plates), and the toddler and

baby were hovering. So before I'm called to duty, I would grab my spade and start chipping into the soil to slice off the weeds by the root, then sling the debris into a wheelbarrow, and dump it at the bottom of the garden to rot down and eventually create a bank.

As the wheelbarrow, with its ever-flattening tyre, kept making the same journey each time, rolling over the thick grass and squashing it, a curvy path had naturally developed (garden design theorists would call this a desire line—a path that naturally occurs when the same route is trodden again and again—but I'll stick with plain old path). I noticed this most clearly when I viewed the garden from upstairs in the house. Just like the gradual transition from seed to plant, so the shape of the garden had begun to form. The area on one side of the path would be the edible garden and on the other side would be the flower garden.

I started to take pictures of the garden whenever I went out and did my quick stint. This was very much a thoughtful moment of "facing north." Yes, I wanted to work quickly to make use of the time. But I would still step back, take a deep breath (it was usually so cold that I could see it), and notice the progress. And each night before I went to sleep, I would look at all the pictures to keep myself feeling positive.

Creating the path—eventually a brick path—instantly made the garden feel smaller (in a good way) and more manageable. Defining a focal point is valuable in the early stages, especially if you've got a wilderness that is making you wonder what to do first. It could be as simple as deciding where you want to put a tree and then pushing a

Dandelion day

If you are faced with a lot of weeds and feel overwhelmed, just choose one weed for the day and decide to remove as many of these plants as you can. So it could be dandelion day or nettle day; then choose another weed another day. Trying to tackle a whole bunch of weeds at once can be tough and if you concentrate on one you are more likely to perfect your technique for getting rid of it.

bamboo cane into the ground where it will go. Dig out a circle around it, flatten the ground for 2m (6.5ft) in each direction so that the cane is visible, and you've begun.

Once you have the focal point, you can connect the dots with other things that you would like in the garden. Mark out an area for a lawn or a pond or a patio by inserting canes to tell you where they will go. Then start clearing ground around them and the garden starts to shrink. It doesn't look like a field of weeds anymore.

The main reason for suggesting this approach is that if all the attention is put on ground clearance and weed removal, then gardening can start to feel tiresome and laborious and it's easy to give up. Make no mistake about it: weeding and clearing rough ground can be hard work. Few gardens are made without a fair bit of truly heavy lifting. But a diet of nonstop weed-battling is not a good prescription for becoming a 30-minutes-a-day gardener. It's like asking someone to join your book club, then telling them that for the next three months you will be reading the electoral roll.

In addition to marking out areas for different purposes, another morale-booster in taming a wilderness is planting things. Clear just a couple of small spaces and add some plants. You'll then find that you want to protect that area and prevent weeds from encroaching. Before you know it, you've cleared more space for more plants. Like planting to clear ground, planting up a large container is also an easy way to add some life and progress to a previously unloved space like an empty patio. Choose some vibrant evergreens such as carex

A view of the garden from upstairs in the house, not long after I moved in.

Easy wins with a wilderness

Find focal points.

Decide on the positioning of prominent garden features such as trees, statues, paths, or buildings and mark them with canes. The garden will instantly feel like yours and look more manageable.

Add plants amid the jungle.

Start planting before you have cleared the whole area. New plants can serve as encouragement if the weeds look daunting and planting some new plants in different places can help divide large areas into more manageable spaces for clearing.

Be open-minded about weeds.

Leave an area wild to encourage wildlife. Designating a wild garden space will save time, offer a fresh perspective, and present the chance to observe the sights and sounds of the natural world when you are taking time to sit and enjoy the garden.

or euonymus and some seasonal flowers and your container becomes the starting point for getting the rest of the space into shape.

The plants begin to grow. Suddenly you don't notice the rest of the weeds. Suddenly you are out there every night or morning making a little more progress. Suddenly it doesn't feel like work. And you think that the person who said you've got a big job on your hands was being rather pessimistic.

An overgrown garden also presents you with an opportunity to truly work with nature by leaving a bit of wilderness intact. Just a small area allowed to grow wild will provide an important place of shelter for insects and other wildlife. It unlocks the potential for wildflowers to produce food for bees, butterflies, and moths. If our garden has a healthy ecosystem, the more likely we are to feel close to nature. I decided to demarcate the ornamental part of the garden from the area allowed to grow wild with a small hedge running along the back of the garden.

The joy of small things

Revel in new beginnings

I love planting small plants. All that potential. All that promise. There is so much growing to witness and to play a helping hand in bringing to fruition. There's the excitement of seeing the plant's progress on each 30-minute stint you spend in the garden. That wonderful, unfathomable, slightly uncomfortable reality of something growing so much yet also unnoticed as we see it every day—like seeing a child every day, looking back at photos from a year ago, and realizing that that moment has gone.

Of course, there's nothing wrong with planting large plants, and when time is at a premium, they are a good way of getting the structure of the garden together instantly. In fact, if you can afford them then I would recommend going large with evergreen plants (just be prepared to water them a lot in the first couple of years). But for me the joy of gardening that makes it a daily habit comes from the development of small things into much bigger ones. I want to check the size of the courgette or zucchini plant when I get home from work, or see if the first flower has appeared.

Planting out small vegetable plants that you have nurtured from seed is an enriching occasion. It is the teenager leaving home to go to university. Yes, you're on hand to help out when the going gets tough but essentially it's their chance to stand on their own two feet and find their own way in the world, as they put down roots and get established.

Small plants need less maintenance than large ones in the first two years after planting.

Plant out young zucchini plants when you think there won't be another frost.

Planting out the vegetables when the risk of frost has passed (standard advice but also an impossible notion to pin to an exact date) is part of a learning curve that teaches us much about ourselves. Do we have the patience to wait and wait or do we get impatient and just get the plants into the ground early in the hope that the weather doesn't take a turn for the worse? If you are impatient, cut off the bottom of some plastic soda bottles so that they're ready to place over the top of your babies if a late frost is forecast.

I also love planting smaller perennial plants. In some ways it's brave to part with your money early in the spring for a plant that's only showing a mere sliver of growth above the compost surface. But you'll get a knowing nod from the nursery owner who sees that you get it. It doesn't look like much, but you know that from acorns, mighty oaks grow. Or from small, rubbery shoots, beautiful sedums will show off vivid late summer flowers and act as landing pads for butterflies.

Another advantage of planting small (and here's where the teenager-at-university analogy may break down) is that smaller plants won't need a lot of looking after. Buying some big bulky, gap-filling plants in summer is something that I've done many times and will do many times again (it's to counterbalance my wife's penchant for buying more crockery). But I will most likely spend the next few weeks just trying to keep them alive as they contend with hot sun, hot soil, and potential dry spells. Young, smaller plants will not be as demanding and will get established more quickly.

Push down the soil in a circle around the edge of the plant with a trowel to make a bowl and then water the plant. All the water will go down to the plant's roots. Then give it a mulch and it should get off to a flying start. But be ready to give any newly planted plant a soak until puddles appear on the soil if more than a week passes without rain in summer.

Finding a comfortable place

Solace in making a place for pondering

The plants that we grow may be living miracles, but if I had a dollar for every lump of concrete that I've had to dig up to plant something in my garden, I would either be a rich man or a poor man who has spent a lot of money. Still, the feeling of those tired, aching limbs after gardening is a satisfying one, and there is also an amazing outcome to look at.

So let's talk about having a comfortable place in the garden where you can sit contentedly with your hands wrapped around a drink and survey the results of a stint of planting or weeding, a place in the garden that you want to return to each time, to enjoy those facing-north moments. Settling on a space that allows you to reflect and recharge is of paramount importance in developing a feeling of belonging in the garden.

I use the word *comfortable* not just referring to a physically cozy place but also to a place where your mind is at rest and you are able to leave all the clutter of life on the backburner. You may find your comfortable place by accident. And it may not be that physically comfortable. For me, finding it happens purely by chance rather than being a deliberate thing. In my previous tiny courtyard garden, my

Having a place to sit and soak up the atmosphere of the garden helps leave the clutter of life behind for a while.

comfortable place was an unlikely one. The back door of the house opened out onto the garden and by standing on the doorstep, I could see the whole space. Leaning against the back door frame with a mug of hot tea in my hand became my comfortable place for taking a few deep breaths and immersing myself in the garden. This would usually be at night when everyone else had gone upstairs and I could take in the sights and sounds of the garden and potter around. We had a light outside by the door which could illuminate the whole place at night regardless of the time of year.

Creating a comfortable place to be in the garden will transform your relationship to it.

This was my metaphorical north-facing time. I would look at how much the plants had grown and how quickly flowers had faded or burst into bloom. It was a time to think about what to add to the garden, what there was too much of, and what had succeeded or failed. When the rain was falling it was also a place for pondering and for enjoying the sights and sounds of the garden, drinking deeply from nature's hosepipe. I find the sound of rain comforting, and if there hadn't been rain for a time, the comfortable place was also where I could rejoice at the thought of some time off from watering.

You might want your comfortable place to be somewhere more obviously physically comfortable than the one in my old garden. I have a friend who uses a swing seat positioned in full sun where I've spent many summer afternoons sinking into soft cushions and wondering why I've never created such a cozy corner in any of my gardens. My only explanation is that my mind turns to plants when I'm in the garden. The beauty of the swing seat, though, is that from its position right next to the back door of the house, you can survey the whole garden and it's easily accessible and always visible from indoors and out.

Take a look at the areas in your garden that are easily accessible and that are easy to view the garden from. Then make room in one of them where you can sit and be comfortable. Creating this special place will transform the garden from just a doing space to a thinking, relaxing, dreaming, *being* space. It will take your relationship with your garden to another level.

If you only have a balcony to garden in, this goal may seem frustrating at first glance and you may yearn for more space, which is only natural once you've got the urge to grow things. But it also may mean that you have a comfortable place indoors from which you can view your entire growing space, which can be a beautiful thing. When I lived in a fourth-floor flat in London with only a small balcony to garden in, it could be seen entirely from indoors which massively helped me keep a connection with the natural world. And instead of spending all my time gazing at the television, I could turn my eyes a few meters to the right and observe the development of the tomatoes and chillies at close quarters. Coming back from work to sit comfortably in my urban living room and gaze at the plants was my way of spending time every day with my garden. This was also where I could truly relax and, eventually, where I became a 30-minutes-a-day gardener without even realizing it.

And regardless of whether your comfortable space is good enough for a holiday resort or just a simple shelter from the rain, having a place to keep returning to, where you can sit or lean and take a deep breath, will make that 30-minutes-a-day habit much easier to get into. To further define the space and make it even more inspiring, try painting your outdoor furniture with a coloured woodstain that matches the colour scheme of the plants nearby, or adding some cushions, throws, or a table runner to complement the surroundings.

Returning to the same spot will also make you appreciate more how things have grown and developed. Your eye will

keep getting drawn to the same plants as they play out their responses to the changing seasons and to your gentle coaxing. Getting to know plants is similar to getting to know people: we have to take the time to notice what helps them thrive and what makes them anxious. Once we do that, maybe we can help them grow.

Finding peace in repetition

Developing enriching routines

Hoeing is a task that will need repeating through the summer in most gardens.

Opposite: Seeing the first rose of summer (in this case 'Boscobel') is a familiar but unpredictable occasion in the garden.

Two words that usually strike fear into me have the opposite effect when it comes to the garden. Here they are both intrinsic parts of creating a feeling of belonging: the two Rs, repetition and routine.

There are so many times in life when I complain about repetition (I won't bore you with the household chores analogy again). I have an aversion to doing the same things over and over. I don't like many of the cultural quirks of holidays that are repeated annually ad nauseam. Please don't make me wear a paper hat on Christmas Day ever again.

But in the garden it's different. I can't wait until it's the time of year to sow climbing beans for the umpteenth time. And I enjoy the window of opportunity for planting soilless bare-rooted trees and roses that comes around each winter when the plants are dormant. The first roses coming into flower each year always marks the welcome point when summer has arrived. And the endless deadheading of roses during the summer never bores me. In short, gardening is full of things that happen each year and things that are done from scratch each year. It is also full of tasks that are carried out several times in the same year.

But there is also a glorious unpredictability among these activities. I may sow the same crops each year on the windowsill, but they don't come up at exactly the same time or get planted on the same date or in the same place. Likewise, they won't grow at the same pace or be ready to flower or harvest at the same time. By sowing I'm not setting in motion a process that will have an exact outcome, like boiling a kettle or making a sandwich. Rather, it is the beauty of being both conductor and audience. The repetition of sowing, weeding, and watering is the framework around which the garden develops, but it is also the way in which we build a lasting connection with the place, as it develops at nature's pace and in nature's time.

The second R is one that in other walks of life I tend to shy away from too. I normally remove four letters and spell routine r-u-t. I don't want to keep doing the same thing at the same time, or on the same day. You'll never find a week-planner on my desk with all the meals and activities noted in advance. I'll never deliberately eat the same thing on the same day of the week because that's just what you do on that day of the week. I like to take life a day at a time and see what happens. Why am I telling you this? Because again, as with repetition, despite initial misgivings, I have ended up

Watering recently planted plants is top of the to-do list after an initial walk around the garden in summer.

Opposite: Deadheading is a satisfying and therapeutic task that will add a lot more flowers to the garden.

fashioning a routine and enjoying the way it is shaped by the unpredictability of tending each garden that I take it to. And because again, this routine may help you to cultivate that feeling of belonging in the garden.

In spring and summer, it goes something like this: before I lift a spade or fork and do any work, I will walk around the garden. I'll check over all the things that have been planted recently and see how they are growing; or if they were recently sowed, then if they have germinated. Ever the unscientific optimist (but serious sleuth), I'll even check the day after sowing. Then I'll look out for what needs watering and make a mental note of weeds that I hadn't spotted before or ones that are becoming troublesome. I'll also keep an eye out for any signs of pests or problems with any plants.

I'll always prioritize the watering, regardless of the time of day. I say this because the ideal time to water is first thing in the morning or in the cool of the evening. But ultimately watering at a less desirable time (midday or early afternoon) is far better than not watering at all, so water while you remember, especially with newly planted plants in summer. Just try not to apply the water directly onto the leaves in hot weather or they can be scorched and lose their colour. A good mulch will also help retain moisture around the base of the plant. A good mulch will also help retain moisture around the base of the plant.

Maybe my eyes will be drawn to the biggest weeds next and I'll impulsively decide to pull them out, followed by snipping off dead flowers to encourage more blooms on favourite flowering plants. This deadheading is important for keeping the garden colourful. Promptly removing spent flowers will in many cases encourage more blooms and will prevent plants from setting seed (although at the end of summer, leaving old flowers intact will allow for the development of attractive berries and seedheads). I also use deadheading as a chance to tidy up the shape of roses and summer-flowering shrubs by removing the flowers and a bit of the stem too if it's making the plant look lopsided.

Then after that, who knows? Often it's many things that I had no idea I would do when I went outside. The initial walk around the garden is not just an exercise in making a mental to-do list. As you see what things need attending to, you'll notice all manner of other things. For instance, which plants are sprinters and which are plodders? Which flowers do the bees keep seeking out, and which ones do they ignore? Where does sunlight fall on the garden? Which plants seem to thrive in shade and which are struggling? The weeds that are the most stubborn. The bird that keeps coming back to the same place. As you do this, the world that has always been right there will begin to enlarge. Every observation unlocks new doors of discovery.

And now that the garden is a place where we belong, it's time to believe in the possibilities.

2

Believing in the garden

Knowing that plants want to grow

Adults were children
Blooming flowers were tiny seeds
Glorious gardens were desolate concrete

A blank canvas
doesn't become a
mature garden over-
night, but the process
is as beautiful as the
end result.

When I meet someone for the first time, the conversation inevitably comes around to the so-what-do-you-do stage, which, if I I'm honest, I try to avoid. Because what follows is an exchange about gardening (no one ever wants to talk about writing) in which the person's response to me is often, "Oh, I haven't got green fingers" or, "Everything that I try to grow just curls up its toes and dies." Then a tale of an early failure is recounted—the story of a houseplant that went from lush and jungle-y to brown and crispy in two weeks or a pot of seeds that decided to stay beneath the compost surface for good. And inevitably comes the poinsettia that turned to a skeleton before the holidays even arrived (you're fortunate if it survived the ride home).

Sadly, negative experiences can easily stick, but they shouldn't define us. Gardening has its pitfalls, but regularly engaging with your growing space by spending a little time in it each day will shift the focus from expecting a plant to die to expecting it to grow. Because in the natural world things grow. And as the garden feels like a place you belong in, so the interest in what makes each plant grow gets stronger. I am sure that most of the time when someone tells me that they can't grow plants, the real problem is that their heart isn't in it.

Whatever the garden looks like now, it won't stay that way. This is my garden in its first year, one picture in spring and one in summer.

Freeing up your mind to believe that plants will grow and that you can help them do it and do it well is a game-changer. It is the foundation of your plans and dreams for the garden.

As well as believing that plants will develop, we also have to believe that whatever we see in our gardens today, it is not the end of the story. Look out of the window at your garden now and I bet there are corners that you want to change or plants that will only start to fulfil their potential in a couple of years' time, maybe longer. Or an overgrown patch that could be a vegetable garden or a patio one day.

As a 30-minutes-a-day gardener, you have to believe in both today and tomorrow. See the beauty of the present and the promise of the future. It's a delicious mix that leaves me walking back indoors as the last moments of light disappear, having delighted in the garden for what it is but also feeling impatient for what it will become.

It's ok if others don't see the potential. I started work on my current garden when the house was also being renovated. The immediate thing that could be seen from inside was a rather large and untidy pile of battered wooden posts, old bathroom fittings, broken plasterboard, and various other unattractive debris. Visitors would ask me, "So, what about the garden then?" which I took to mean, "What are you doing about the mess, seeing as you're the gardener of the house?"

My next thought was a defensive, "Have you any idea how much I've done already?" But on reflection, I felt that these remarks were understandable. My hours of clearing and tidying and the picture in my head of what the place would look like in the future were lost on anyone else but me. On first glance, the garden looked messy and like a big problem, especially to the untrained eye, and perhaps yours does right now too. But it doesn't matter: it looks completely different if you believe.

Should it stay or should I hoe?

Seeing weeds in a new light

Believing in the potential of a garden can be difficult if you have an abundance of weeds or if the garden is so overgrown that it needs some serious groundwork to get it back to a blank canvas. But taking a tolerant approach to weeds can undo the anxiety that these unwanted plants bring on. In fact, that's the nail hit squarely on the head: if a weed is an unwanted plant and unwanted plants are a major headache, perhaps it's time to see more of them as wanted plants. Do this and you will instantly have a lot fewer weeds in your garden.

I was out in the garden one spring afternoon with my eldest son when he was a toddler and as usual, he was busy prioritizing his tasks while I was busy tackling mine. Apparently picking off sedum stems and putting them in a basin of water to "give them a bath" is a serious task in the garden for a two-year-old. Over time I've come to learn that our tasks in the garden are each equally important. As much as I wanted to make progress with my latest path, planting area, or vegetable crop, I needed to let him discover the outdoors for himself without expecting him to have an innate enthusiasm for starting a new row of beetroot plants from seed.

It was with this arrangement in place that I noticed him walking around carrying a bamboo cane while I was doing some planting. He was using the cane to hit some of the plants, saying, "Naughty

Is that weed a friend or foe?

Some non-native plants are classed as invasive, having the potential to spread rapidly and to threaten endemic plant species in the wild, and their habitats. If you've spotted something growing like crazy in your garden that you didn't plant, check with your local authority for a list of invasive plants in your area to see if it's one of them. It can be an offence to intentionally grow non-native invasives so if you've got one, prioritize its removal.

plant, naughty plant." After responding with a mixture of laughter and frustration when I noticed some raspberry canes rather worse for wear after their beating, I started to direct him to the weeds, explaining which plants were truly naughty. But then it dawned on me that getting frustrated about weeds was pointless. A plant cannot be naughty just for having the audacity to grow. This awareness has also challenged my understanding of when a child is and isn't being naughty.

Rather than advocating letting your garden turn into a wilderness, my point is that if you are clearing a garden and it's not possible to quickly get rid of unwanted plants, embrace them until you have the time, money, or other resources to replace them with something else. Don't stress yourself by seeing them as naughty plants. Some of these so-called problem plants, such as creeping thistle, have brought pest-eating ladybirds (or ladybugs) to my garden in good numbers.

Sometimes finding long periods of time to devote to gardening is difficult. It certainly is for me, especially when family life gets chaotic, but I have learned that while some tasks may require several hours of work to complete, it is fruitless to worry about them in the meantime. Is it really the end of the world if an untidy corner stays untidy for a few weeks more? It is also worth bearing in mind that if you don't have time to completely clear areas of weeds, you can still keep them in check. A quick ten minutes of slicing off a few of the biggest weeds or pulling out thistle seedlings in spring soon adds up if it becomes a daily habit.

Now don't get me wrong: some weeds can be troublesome. The way that the spindly vines of field bindweed infiltrate the centre of some of my plants and place them in a chokehold is nothing short of annoying. They also try to invade the gaps in the brickwork of our house, but that's another story.

Then there's the ability of stinging nettles to find the one sliver of naked flesh that is available. Why does that always happen? If like me you wear ripped jeans in the garden, then you will know what I mean. It requires vigilance to stop these climbing or stinging suspects from invading other plants.

Keep reminding yourself, "What's the worst that could happen?" if an overgrown patch of the garden is bothering you. In the context of your other plants, the worst that could happen is that weeds suffocate things that you have planted and stop them from growing well. If the weeds are non-native invasives, you may have no choice but to get rid of them. But otherwise, this leads nicely to what I think may be the best way to turn a wilderness into the growing space that you've always wanted.

Planting is the best form of weeding. We can completely clear weeds from a space in the garden, but if we don't have anything to sow or plant in it and it was just a tidiness or control exercise, then the weeding will need to be done all over again.

I started overhauling the wilderness in my garden by clearing a few spaces where I wanted to plant things and putting new plants in. Gradually as I started protecting the area around each plant by hoeing off the surrounding weeds, the expanses of untamed ground between plants started to disappear and the garden began to take shape almost without my realizing it. It was like putting together separate elements of a jigsaw and then discovering that just a few more pieces could connect them all together.

Finding the right place

Understanding where to plant what

If you're getting the idea that plants want to grow in your garden, then a little experimentation is a natural next step. What do I mean by this? Well, you may have heard the saying, "Right plant, right place." The idea is that if you have clay soil, grow a plant that likes clay. This of course makes perfect sense

'Princess Anne' is a healthy, scented rose that grows surprisingly well in shade.

and can save a lot of frustration and disappointment. Maybe some of the people who have told me their tales of planting woe had tried to grow an acid-loving blueberry in chalky soil. Or a bog-loving astilbe in dry, stony soil.

However, once you believe in the plants in your garden and witness at close quarters the powerful force of growth (which is unmissable if you find time each day to sit in your comfy place and observe your plants), then it seems only natural to want to see how far nature's boundaries can be pushed.

Ok, it might not seem natural to you, but if so, there is still likely to be a scenario where you fall in love with a plant that you see in a nursery or a plant centre and have to take home. Is there the perfect home for it in your garden? Maybe, maybe not, but is it waiting for perfection or is it happy to put up with a few privations? The only way to find out is to plant it and see.

Don't get me wrong: if a plant had cost a lot of money, it makes sense to have suitable conditions for it, so that you can roll out the red carpet and give it the star treatment that your investment deserves. Yet few growing condition requirements are life or death matters for plants. This reminds me of visiting a lavender farm in the UK and talking to the owners about their soil. I'd read all the textbook requirements for lavender, with free-draining soil being number one on the list. This particular place had quite a heavy soil, although admittedly it was stony. But the lavender thrived, and if you visited in midsummer, you could have been forgiven for thinking that you were in Provence.

It is by being willing to live a little and give plants a chance that we discover so much more about them. In a

Acorus 'Ogon' is an evergreen grass that likes to be kept damp.

previous garden I grew several shrub roses in some heavily shaded areas that received small amounts of sun. One of them was 'Princess Anne', a real unusual treasure of a rose, with flowers that seem to show every conceivable shade of purple, a few reds, and, as the flowers age, an audacious flash of yellow. It responded with at least three flushes of flowers a year and the glossiest, healthiest leaves that I had in the garden.

There are times when it pays not to rebel with your choices, especially if a plant needs an extreme. I don't take any chances with acid- or chalk-loving plants. My soil is clay and alkaline, so I don't even attempt to grow blueberries, rhododendrons, or pieris in it. Trying to grow these plants in alkaline soil is like trying to feed a vegan a beefburger. It's a futile exercise.

But if a planting guide says that a plant requires full sun and you only have sun for half a day, why not give it a go? Being a rebellious planter is all part of the learning process of believing in the garden. It can also take the urge to nurture a step further. Ok, so maybe your soil is slightly drier than is ideal for a particular plant: you can use it as an opportunity to pay more attention to this plant, which could be, say, a moisture-loving *Acorus* 'Ogon'. It likes to be damp, so here's an opportunity to check it for watering a couple of times a week to make sure that it's well-mulched in spring, and to admire more often the beautiful, arching habits of its glossy strands that make it such a valuable evergreen.

There's no need to be reckless or wasteful with what you plant where, but dare to be just a little bit different. Sometimes when we encourage a friend to push their boundaries, we develop a much deeper, longer-lasting relationship than we ever thought possible.

Moving plants

Like moving house, it might be stressful,
but it's worth the effort

The big breakthrough in believing happened for me when I realized that plants could be moved from one place to another and that they could grow in the place that they had been moved to. I had a teacher at college who was always moving plants in the college grounds. He used to tell us that if you weren't happy with the position of a plant, then you should move it. He would even move plants just a few inches if he thought they weren't quite in the right place. While this is a drastic example (and the plants were small if I remember rightly), it spurred me on to try it for myself. Now I challenge myself to see how late in spring I can successfully move something. It's the closest that I get to living on the edge!

Moving a plant for the first time feels very different to planting, even though the two scenarios are similar if the plant that you are moving has been in its original place for less than a year. There is something of the amateur surgery about moving a plant: getting out the cutting tools, cutting off the plant's life support mechanism (the roots), and transporting it without so much as an anaesthetic.

I started with moving roses. I remember the first one. My parents had a species rose—*Rosa rubrifolia*—in their garden that over the years had become entangled with couch grass. This is a very persistent spreading grass that takes no prisoners, although in a way it kind of had by growing in the centre of this rose and stealing all the moisture, like an uninvited guest who eats all the food and never wants to leave no matter how many hints you drop. A few spindly stems of the rose were clinging to life, but it was not happy and there didn't seem to be much to lose.

Moving the beautiful *Rosa rubrifolia* in winter to help it thrive in summer was an early experiment for me in moving plants.

After I chopped a rather crude square into the soil around the plant and levered up the clods of thick, airless clay soil, the whole thing came up, complete with couch grass. Holding these two uprooted plants that were packed together, I was able to pull the clump of couch grass out of the centre of the rose, like a dentist who prized out a tooth to relieve a patient of toothache. Without a big clump of grass growing through it, the rose clearly had potential. It was winter (the best time to move roses), so there was time to hold the plant in some kind of smug triumph (I am easily pleased) as if it was—to switch images—a hefty salmon reeled in from freshwater. I planted it into its slightly sandier new home about a hundred feet away and seeing it start to grow the following spring was an epiphany. It flowered like never before and after the hot pink blossoms, there are dark red rose hips to accompany the unusual smoky-blue leaves.

HOW TO MOVE A PLANT, STEP-BY-STEP

_____

If you are moving a plant in spring, do it in the morning or evening when conditions are cooler and ideally when rain is imminent. Avoid moving plants in summer unless temperatures are going to be below 15°C (60°F) for a few days, but even then it's very risky. If it's winter, woody plants such as roses can be cut back after they've been moved to encourage lots of new growth.

Before you start to move the plant, dig the hole where you want the plant to be moved to, so that the moved plant won't stay out of the soil for long. Start by loosening the soil around the edge of the plant (at about the plant's width away from its centre) with a garden fork. Start tentatively, loosening all the way around the plant, then slowly start to lever up the fork. If you can feel the roots pulling, keep levering the fork all the way around the plant, making sure to push the fork deep into the soil each time. If the roots aren't pulling, loosen the soil a bit closer to the centre of the plant.

Once the roots have been loosened all the way around, try to gently lift the plant from the ground by holding onto the soil around the rootball. This will either result in the plant coming out, or expose any roots that are still clinging on. Dig further down if roots are still intact. If it isn't feasible to dig all the way to the bottom, trim off the root with a pair of secateurs or pruners.

Hold the plant by the rootball rather than its stems and drop it into the planting hole. If the hole isn't big enough, resist the urge to squash it in (it can be a strong urge, but you can fight it!). Make the hole wider or deeper as necessary, so that the roots comfortably fit in the hole.

Once the plant is in its new spot in the garden, water it very well until puddles form on the soil surface, then mulch the plant with a couple of spadefuls of well-rotted compost. Keep watering in dry spells for the first two years.

Plants can be successfully moved if they aren't growing in the ideal position.

Every plant is a miracle in its own way. Whether it's a weed that goes unnoticed behind the trash cans, a beautiful cherry tree in full bloom, or this quirky blue-leaved rose that yearned to be free, every plant has a strong urge to grow. And thanks to my teacher, I realized that just like us, plants have the ability to make someone's day a bit brighter. But some of them get stuck and need a helping hand in order to reach their potential.

More for less

Dividing plants, the ultimate freebie

As our belief in plants grows, so our confidence and growing skills do too. Gardening is a strange pursuit in some ways because to bring out the best in many of the plants that we grow, an act of sabotage or brutality has to be carried out on them. This is where we learn so much about the resilience of our plants but also about ourselves. Have we got the nerve to slice a spade through our best perennials? Or prize them apart with a pair of forks? If you can dive headlong into this, then the 30-minute habit is paying off. Because let's face it, it sounds pretty violent, doesn't it? Chopping a plant into sections after removing it from its home where it was doing nicely, thanks for asking?

But to divide a plant is to revive a plant. That old sedum that shows off some pretty flowers for the butterflies at the end of summer has the potential to be a family of young ones, ready to leave the comfort of the mother plant and bring a fresh vitality to the garden. Think of an old, congested clump of perennials (you may have inherited some of these when you moved in). I like to think of them as ageing rock stars.

You know how it goes: a once high-profile act whose influence is dwindling, their importance fading as newer, younger stars take centre stage. If only someone would rattle their cage, break them out of their comfort zone, and push them into new areas.

This is how it is with dividing plants. As many perennials get older, their display of flowers starts to dwindle and they just don't take centre stage in the garden anymore. If allowed to get bigger and bigger, taking up more and more room in the garden while flowering tails off with each passing year, they are set to drift into obscurity. This is the time to divide them.

If you can identify a plant like that in your garden now, here's a good test of where you are at in believing. Would you happily dig it up, rip it into sections, and replant them? Does it sound too painful or destructive? It will be the best thing you ever did.

For me, it has been the things in life that I have dreaded the most that have ended up making me a stronger, more colourful character, and so it is with plants. Dividing them may seem like a drastic thing to do, but it will give them a new lease on life. If you've visited a public garden with a large herbaceous border and wondered how on earth everything can have its allotted space and be so full of flowers and fresh growth, the answer is that the gardeners there divided plants and believed.

HOW TO DIVIDE YOUR PLANTS, STEP-BY-STEP

Spring is the best season for dividing plants in the garden, although it can be done in fall too. In spring you can also divide young plants that you've just bought. It's a great way of getting two, three, or maybe four plants for the price of one (with apologies to nursery owners, but I also recommend buying lots of plants!).

Plan where you want to put newly divided plants and dig the planting holes before you begin.
Especially with a larger plant, this will save you from frantically trying to find room while all the new divisions are exposed and slowly wilting (a sad situation, believe me). Wait until at least one new shoot has appeared on plants such as bergenia if the fibrous roots have been chopped into clumps with a spade.

Plant all divisions immediately after extracting them from the soil.
Or if you can't plant straightaway, plunge them into a bucket of water in a shady corner—but don't leave them there any longer than an hour.

Use a pruning saw or breadknife to divide very old clumps of perennials.
It can be difficult to separate large clumps of hemerocallis (daylilies), for example. Otherwise, plants with fibrous roots are best divided by placing two forks back to back in the middle of the clump and pushing them away from each other to separate the plants.

Or be selective!
Don't feel as if you need to find room for ten of the same plant just because you have a big clump to divide. Plant as many new divisions as you think are necessary to blend with the surrounding plants, then pot up and give away or compost the ones that you don't have room for.

1. This potted *Stachys* 'Hummelo' is easily split into two. Make sure that the plant is watered before tipping it from its pot and holding the roots ready to be divided.

2. Continue to hold the plant and, starting near the bottom, press your thumbs into the compost and slowly pull your hands away from you to loosen the roots. As the plant begins to separate, move your hands upward and keep gently pulling the rootball (trying not to pull the fragile, young stems).

3. Immediately plant each new division, firm it in well with your hands, and water in well. Each division should have a few strong shoots. If not, plant a couple together in the same hole. Small divisions can take a long time to bulk up and make a notable plant.Keep watering in dry spells for the first spring and summer.

3

Becoming a 30-minutes-a-day gardener

A wondrous journey

Tuning in to nature
Leaning in to listen harder
Losing track of time
Finding a new way

Grasses flowering in
summer, an annual
hay fever trigger.

Many things in life happen every year that still somehow manage to take me by surprise. Does this happen to you? The start of the hay fever season is one for me. Every summer since I was 18, I've gotten hay fever symptoms when native grasses start to flower in mid-June. And every year I forget, eventually taking tablets and kicking myself that I didn't remember this annual event early enough to avoid the symptoms that follow.

A similar thing can happen with gardening. In a climate that has four seasons, the landscape changes so much in a calendar year. If your relationship with the garden is a casual and occasional one, then there is a good chance that a lot of regular occurrences will take you by surprise, and opportunities will pass you by. All of a sudden, the lawn is growing strongly, when the last time you looked, it appeared dormant. Or maybe there was a chance to sow some fruiting vegetables in late spring, but when we remembered, the moment was gone, and some rather sorry-looking plants are all that remain in the garden centre, the ones that nobody else wants.

None of this need apply though as you become a 30-minutes-a-day gardener. If the garden is an ever-present part of life, then so are the reminders of how the seasons change and the opportunities that each presents. You will be watching for what to sow next, what can safely be planted outside, and what is ready to harvest.

Still, everyone (especially me) needs reminders about some things: intuition about when to do what in the garden can take years to develop. Consider, for example, the standard advice to plant after the last frost. This rather strange and perhaps confusing statement requires the ability to see into the future. Which frost will turn out to be the last one? But as you become

When you watch the garden develop closely, you will appreciate even the smallest of changes in a plant.

absorbed in the daily habit of gardening, you will find yourself checking the weather forecast to see if it's going to be cold at night. You'll feel that it might be too much of a shock to plant out that courgette tonight; best wait a couple of days when temperatures should be much milder. Or you'll get the feeling that it's the right time to sow salads in late spring, when a few days' break from heavy rain has made the puddles disappear and the soil dry enough to be broken up without becoming a mud pie.

Your garden diary can help

The beauty of seeing results

While you are in the process of sharpening your gardening skills, keeping some sort of garden diary will prove to be invaluable. Whether it's in a good old-fashioned, hardcopy diary, a cellphone app, or an Instagram account, recording the progress of the garden is a great habit to get into—it goes hand-in-hand with the 30-minutes-a-day-in-the-garden lifestyle. Your phone is perhaps the most convenient medium, but when I take time indoors to reflect on the garden, I start to dream and plan for the future. This usually involves sketching plans and jotting notes in a notebook—one with graph paper is my favourite tool.

Keeping a garden diary is also an investment in your future gardening endeavours. A record of what you sowed when, and when you harvested, will continue to be a handy reference in the following years. It will help you to understand how long crops take to mature, and how many days a tiny annual seed needs to make the transition from seedling to flowering plant. As you get into the process, you may find yourself adding lots of extra details such as extremes of weather, wildlife spotted in the garden, pests that you noticed, and what they did to your plants. Building up your own resource of gardening experiences is to lay down a solid foundation for the rest of

Taking pictures from the same place over time helps you to see how the garden has developed and changed.

your gardening life. Of course, the beauty of the great outdoors is that no two years are ever the same and no plant will ever behave exactly the same way each year. But having a daily record of a year in the garden will arm you with some hard evidence of what happened the year before, even when your mind wants to play tricks with you and swear blind that it has no knowledge at all of the matter at hand (or of the hay fever).

Beyond recording a year's worth of tasks in your own garden, maybe the most significant benefit of keeping a garden diary comes from the continuous visual record that you can create. Just like pets, children, and overdrafts, gardens seem to grow bigger by stealth, and we can fail to notice the extent of the changes until something reminds us how small they once were.

Being able to look back on those photos you've taken of the garden every day should help you to appreciate how much progress you've made, and dampen down any discouragement. Like the irresistible allure of before-and-after photos on Instagram, when you look back at what the garden looked like in winter when it's summer, a pictorial record of transformation becomes a powerful thing. And now that you are in the habit of spending that precious half hour in the garden and of keeping track, whether by phone or notebook, of the wondrous way that things develop, you are truly becoming a gardener. Next come the endless possibilities.

Endless possibilities

When gardening ceases to be a fight

Did you sometimes used to think of gardening as a fight? Human versus giant weeds. Human versus concrete. Human versus windy balcony. Human versus rotting decking. Me against the clock. That's how it feels if your connection to the garden is loose and time spent out there is only in response to a problem that can't be ignored anymore. But as you become a gardener and have a daily connection with the place, gardening becomes a more peaceful pastime of projects, pottering, and play rather than a battleground.

If you are anything like me as a gardener, you may find yourself sitting out in the garden in your comfortable place enjoying a morning coffee. Then you have an idea. And before you know it, there's a new garden project underway before the cup's empty. That's the great thing about being on top of things in the garden and taking time to just sit and enjoy it. This way there's room for spontaneity and creativity.

The scale of the project might be small. Perhaps it's planting succulents into the cracks in a concrete patio or patio wall, digging up some leggy plants that are past their best, or painting a fence panel in a fetching shade of blue. The more time that I spend taking stock of the garden, just sitting in it and seeing it for what it is, the more the ideas come, and the place gets refined.

Laying the main brick path for the garden was a major task in my garden but I tackled it a little bit at a time.

Maybe you're sitting out in the garden and decide that something drastic needs to be done to enhance it, perhaps a new patio or a reconfiguration of the borders, or perhaps a green roof on the shed. Even if all you have is 30 minutes at a time, such an ambitious project is still feasible.

I started laying a brick path in the garden in the first winter after we moved in. We had heavy snow in February and I remember looking out at the garden from upstairs and watching the shallow trench that I had started to chip out with a spade slowly disappear as the snow filled it in. Fast forward to the end of June and it's midsummer. I'm upstairs opening the windows and as I look out onto the garden, I'm momentarily surprised to see that the path is only half finished. But then I notice progress: calendulas and strawberries edge the finished part, and further away are potatoes in flower, roses in bud, and beans beginning to set pods.

Why am I painting this picture of the garden and the path-to-be? To emphasize that the process can still be enjoyed even when time is at a premium and that big jobs can still be tackled even if you only spend half an hour a day in the garden. Yes, the work is yet to be completed, but I had laid around 200 bricks and, like the path, the garden was heading in the right direction.

A few people had called the half-finished path the road to nowhere. My only response was a wry smile. Quite the opposite. Building the path was a gradually unfolding process that in a strange way mirrored the growth of the plants around it. And while it's nice to accomplish some things quickly, watching construction and living things growing together seemed kind of neat. And besides, it wasn't the road to nowhere. Even if you've only got half a path, no walk taken in the garden is ever a wasted journey.

Prioritizing time and space

Deciding what we want to grow

As you become a gardener, it is highly probable that you will develop a problem. I have it, and I know that I share it with many others. It goes something like this: you are out somewhere and unexpectedly hit upon a stall selling plants. You have to take a couple to save them from their captivity inside a woefully inadequate plastic pot. Next, you pop down to the local nursery for a bag of daffodil bulbs and come back with three evergreen shrubs, two dahlias, some onion sets, and a few leggy herbs that were lurking in the bargain bin, hoping and praying for a careful owner to give them another chance.

Why is this a problem? Well, it isn't necessarily but I sometimes get carried away in the moment and think with my heart, not my head. So here comes the boring part, offered not to lecture but to help you enjoy your garden as much as possible. If time and space are limited, ask yourself this question: what do I really want to grow? Then take out that soil-smeared notepad where you scribble down your garden diary notes and start your list. Once you are confident that you've thought of everything (impossible, I know), look at the available space

Left to right:

Small cracks in concrete are the perfect home for succulent plants such as *Sedum sediforme* 'Silver'. Other succulents suitable for growing like this include *Sempervivum calcareum*, *Sedum album* 'Coral Carpet', and *Sedum tetractinum* 'Coral Reef'.

Break up the rubble and soil at the base of the crack, then lower in your plant. Any crack that the roots can be squeezed into will be large enough.

Check the planting depth, making sure that the base of the plant's stems is just above ground level.

Fill any gaps with a sprinkling of gritty compost and firm it in gently with your hand. Also sprinkle grit over the compost to improve drainage and to create a decorative mulch.

30-MINUTES-A-DAY-
FOR-A-WEEK PROJECT IDEAS

In just a half hour a day, you can open up more growing space and personalize it too.

Plant up some cracks in a patio.
Avoid treading over the plant and in a few weeks, you should notice signs of growth. If it is very hot and dry for a few days in the first couple of months after planting, water the base of the plant well.

Replace hard surfaces with green space and permeable materials.
If you long for more growing space and have the opportunity, think about chipping away at the amount of concrete and other hard surfaces that you have. A sledgehammer and pickaxe will be enough to break up most concrete surfaces. This project doesn't have to be a full-scale demolition job and that may not be feasible anyway. Bear in mind that even a small space will generate a large pile of rubble.

Before you begin, always check first to see if there are any drain covers close to the area that you want to change, and seek advice from a professional if you are worried about disturbing utility lines.

If the thought of having rubble to dispose of at the end is a worry, you could crush it up with a sledgehammer and use the beaten-up rubble as the base for a new patio or path somewhere else in the garden. Or if you advertise it, someone will like the idea of free path foundations.

Make a raised bed.
Raised beds can be handy additions to the garden, although it's worth thinking about whether they are really the right thing for you. For example, filling

them up requires a lot of compost or soil, so dedicating a large growing area to raised beds can be time consuming and expensive.

Raised beds are valuable if:

- Your soil is heavy and you want to add a thick new layer of topsoil to grow plants that need finer soil (root vegetables, for instance).
- You have an overgrown area and want to quickly demarcate part of it to show some encouraging progress.
- The soil depth is shallow and plants are constantly drying out and struggling in warm spells.
- When you mark out a raised bed, make sure that you can reach easily into all of it without having to walk inside the bed, which would damage the soil structure and compromise drainage.
- If you decide to use wood, make sure that the soil at the base of the joining posts and the main boards has had a good helping of gravel mixed into it to allow water to escape quickly. This will prolong the life of the wood by reducing the likelihood of rotting.

Paint an outside wall.

If the terms of your living arrangement allow it, painting an exterior wall is a great way of setting the tone for the style of your garden. It is also a useful way of emphasizing a colour scheme in the garden. Masonry paints are available in a range of colours that can transform your patio area or back-door planting space. A warm shade of orange would suit a jungle-y garden of tropical exotics, while a white wall would suit a south-facing, Mediterranean courtyard planted with lavenders and olives.

and see if carrying out your wish list is feasible. If not, maybe it's time for a garden project that will open up more space.

What am I getting at here? When time and space are limited, the garden will be far more enriching if we grow things that we really like rather than just things that we are managing to keep alive. Of course, part of the journey of becoming a gardener is that we learn to love plants over time. Maybe some favourites will be plants that you weren't sure of at first but that you've become attached to as you care for them and observe their quirks on a daily basis.

I never really gave blueberries the time of day until I started growing one in a pot and was amazed by the rich and dramatic range of fall shades that it displayed in October. I had thought the plant's usefulness had passed long ago when the birds ate all its fruit in July. Now they are among my favourite plants, and I would grow them purely for their ornamental value. I've never had the very acidic soil that they demand (ideally a pH of 5 or lower), so I have always had to grow them in pots of ericaceous compost, but they are worth the effort and the space.

Even bearing in mind the possibility of our being converted to a certain plant, our gardens are likely to be more rewarding places if the starting point for choosing plants is a personal wish list. This is especially the case with edible plants. It is so easy to make buying decisions that will eat away at your space but leave you with little that you yourself want to eat. Before you know it, that gourmet vegetable patch can be filled up by just a small bag of seed potatoes and a bag of onion sets. Instead, think about what you like to eat the most and check that they are suitable for your climate. I asked my wife to tell me what she liked eating the most so I could grow it in the garden. Unfortunately, mangos, oranges, and guavas aren't designed for the UK's cool, wet winters, so we had to prioritize crops that were less exotic, such as beetroot and climbing French beans.

It's also the same with ornamental plants. Ok, you've seen a bargain, but does it fit in with the style or theme of the rest of the garden? If you think I'm being picky, ask yourself if you would buy a chair that didn't go with your couch or carpet. Apply the same selective approach to choosing plants for the garden and you will develop a more satisfying space. (If you are the kind of person who would buy a chair that doesn't go with the couch, then ignore me—I admire your spirit.)

Growing crops and flowers that we are ambivalent about is a slippery slope and surely the cause of disillusionment for some who then may never become gardeners. Remember that anecdote where everyone wants to share their gardening woes? I can guarantee that over the years I've heard plenty of stories about resentful relationships that began with an unloved plant that was bequeathed by the previous owners. The solution is to get rid of it and grow what you want to grow.

As well as providing luscious fruits, blue-berries have fantastic fall foliage colour.

Don't feel guilty

Nature will help if you miss a day

Once you're in the habit of engaging daily with what's happening in the garden, going away in spring or summer when so much is growing can be a wrench even if it's only for a day or two. A couple of days in early summer can change a garden a lot; leave for a week and the change is vast. This is when I walk into the garden, give it a withering look, and say, "I thought I knew you . . ." Perhaps it's that feeling that I've missed out on something, or that things would have been more ordered if I had been here, and now the place is looking a bit loose around the edges. Weeds that I swear weren't there when I left now look two months old, never mind two days. Roses that were about to burst into flower have already peaked and the flowers are starting to lose their crispness.

Over time, I've learned to be more relaxed about taking time off. I can do a lot to mitigate the problem of being away from the garden in summer. I can move thirsty pots to shade, soak and mulch the young, recently planted plants, and save hanging baskets in a cool corner—all good things to keep plants ticking over a forecasted hot spell. But I can't play God, and the truth is that the garden will be just fine. If anything, seeing the garden looking a little unkempt after we've been away is a reminder of how much growth we just don't notice when we are around day after day. And the garden is fine without me for a bit. Maybe it's been longing for me to stop fussing around and to just be left alone.

The aim of this observation is to say you should not beat yourself up if you miss a couple of days in the garden. It will forgive you. Don't feel like you've failed. You'll probably have that twinge of disappointment if you do have to spend some days away from the garden during the growing season, but this is healthy because it's when you know you've become a gardener.

4

When all the world is sleeping

Winter

Muddy boots
Frosted leaves
Low sun
Tired weeds
Absent friends
Hopes and dreams

Old seedheads on grasses and perennials look beautiful when lit by low winter sun.

So here I am in the garden on a winter's afternoon. I'm surrounded by remnants of the weeds that had got a foothold during summer. When we took over our new home in fall, the garden was a wilderness so neglected that there was almost no natural light indoors, the windows blocked by a thicket of old buddlejas.

Fortunately, messing about in the garden in winter isn't something that I just started doing when I had an overgrown new garden to tackle. As I've mentioned, it's always been part of my life, along with the great feeling of sliding out of your muddy boots, removing your dirty socks, and sitting down indoors with a warm drink, aching limbs, and the good tiredness that comes from a stint of winter gardening. Yes, there may be little daylight, it may be cold out there, and signs of life may be hard to find. Yet winter can offer a window of opportunity for the 30-minutes-a-day gardener.

For some of us, this will be a larger window than for others since the scope of what we can accomplish depends largely on how severe the winter is. Perhaps you have snow and frost covering the ground, leaving the garden unworkable for months. If so, some of my favourite winter tasks may need to wait. Winters where I live, close to the coast in north-eastern England, tend to be light on snow and frost but so wet that the soil isn't in any state for planting or weeding for long periods of time. If the vagaries of climate suggest taking a break, you can experience your half hour of quality gardening time indoors.

But if the ground isn't frozen or waterlogged (and sometimes even if it is), a lot can be accomplished. "What exactly?" I hear you asking. Let's take a look at what we can achieve.

Taking stock and clearing ground

How winter makes it easier

Sometimes during summer, I look back at pictures of the garden in winter and what I always notice first is how flat and empty the place looks—but in a good way. It feels under control, and if the garden was running away from you in the summer, winter brings more breathing space. In winter, those overgrown edges of the garden tend to be trodden and flat, and the vegetable garden has lots of empty gaps. This resetting of the landscape can allow you to think clearly about the garden. There is no fretting about new weeds that need to be pulled out, thirsty crops that need water, or scruffy grass that needs mowing.

Winter provides us with a chance to take stock and to hatch up more plans and schemes about what we want the place to be. The garden in winter is like an item of furniture that has been stripped of its paint and sanded back to the original wood. That's what the changing seasons do. The roses have lost their flowers and most of their leaves, deciduous trees are transformed from pretty umbrellas to stark skeletons. But just like that old sanded down table, the current state is just an opportunity for something beautiful to be born again. And a half hour in the garden is arguably more productive now than in spring or summer.

Clearing ground is a job that I've done during many winters, whether in my own garden, other people's gardens, on my old allotment, or in a community garden. If it's not freezing or too wet, winter is a great time to make headway. There is no battling with heat, hefty weeds, and hard summer ground. We can sense that nature is having a break as the strong pull of the wild has ceased: there won't be an army of fresh new weeds to remove a week after you've cleared a bit of space.

Clearing ground to make new borders and to mark out some garden structures, a path, or a patio is so much easier in winter. When the ground isn't too wet (if it's not sticking to my shoes), nature cuts us a bit more slack. What do I mean? Well, unfrozen ground is less likely to be rock hard in winter even if it's clay soil. In summer, this is a big problem in my garden, and if you have clay soil, you will know what I mean. If you are not sure whether you have clay soil, you can easily find out. If there is clay in it, you will be able to press a small handful into a shape with your thumb, even in summer when it's dry.

It was winter when I started to shape the main paths in my garden. The spade went in easily as I chopped into the soil to make a rough shape. Then I chipped into the ground horizontally in thin layers to remove the old grass. Again, this was easier in winter. I was only doing a small amount each day so that there were many days of path digging. But the grass wasn't growing, so I wasn't faced with a meadow to hack back as I worked my way through.

The garden in its winter state is when the veil has been lifted. It is easier to see its shape and layout and to work out how it can be improved. If you can view the garden from upstairs, keep looking at it from a height in winter. It's much easier to get a feel for the arrangement of the place. Maybe you've seen those sports coaches who choose to sit up in the stands and watch their team play rather than view it from pitchside? I guess it's a bit like that. It's easier to see the bigger picture from a higher vantage point.

Winter is also a naturally good time to work on clearing ground and marking out new spaces because there aren't as many distractions. I don't know about you, but on a glorious summer's day, I am a very easily distracted gardener. Sometimes I go out with a particular task in mind, then do a dozen other things and completely forget what I went out for. It's easily done when the garden is at full throttle and so much is changing so quickly. There are weeds bursting out, hopefully

I cleared my garden a little at a time through winter using hand tools only. Winter allows for this gradual approach, with weeds not growing rampantly to undo your work.

crops doing the same thing too, and so many exciting things to observe and absorb. Winter is different. Just being outside at all can feel like an act of defiance, a move against the tide, because at face value there isn't necessarily much obvious to entice you outdoors for 30 minutes. Sticking to the job that you went out for becomes much easier.

Picturing the scene

Thinking of summer in winter

We've already considered looking at wintry pictures of the garden in summer; doing the reverse is a useful tactic in winter. The summer can soon become a distant memory, and as crops are cleared away, herbaceous plants die down, and trees lose their leaves, it can be hard to reflect on what the garden was like in its full glory. Which plants were taking up too much room, which struggled in shade, and which seemed to desire more room in their pot and will need moving up a size next spring?

Flicking through summer photos of the garden in winter is definitely time well spent, and for me, it serves a similar function as "facing north" does in summer. This is because in winter, there will inevitably be days when spending half an hour in the garden just isn't possible. Maybe you leave for work and get back from work in the dark. I used to do this when I had a long train commute to London, and I would sometimes doze off in the train, then wake up with it still being dark, and for a moment, I wouldn't be sure if I was on the way to work or on the way home. Then there are those inevitable moments when the weather makes gardening impractical or impossible. This is your chance to spend half an hour dreaming of your future hopes for the garden—to take a look at spring or summer photos of the garden and transport yourself back; to reflect on how the garden evolved, and how abundance creeps up by stealth, even when you are keeping a close eye on things on a daily basis.

Think back over the past year in the garden while looking at photos, and not only is it an opportunity to be filled with hope that spring will follow winter, it is also an effective way to get inspired about the changes you can make to the place.

If your garden is new or you've only just started and don't have any old photos, immerse yourself in images of other people's gardens to get inspired. Thirty minutes a day will whizz by (especially if you are looking at pictures on a phone, where time seems to get eaten away greedily, as if a child were devouring a marshmallow). Save pictures that relate to your garden, plants that you would like to find out more about, and design tricks that you think will work in your space. Keeping up a daily habit of 'being a gardener' for 30 minutes is achievable in winter if you do this on inclement days.

Winter is a great opportunity to dig into gardening books. If you are fortunate enough to have people asking you what you would like as a festive gift, point them in the direction of some inspirational garden reading, and even the darkest days can be spent immersing yourself in the garden. Trust me, it will serve as some very refreshing relief from indigestion.

The beauty of taking time to look back on pictures of your garden during the winter months is that it is easier to see the place for what it is. In the moment of summer, it might seem like a good idea to let self-sown plants run riot and invade other plants, but in the cold light of a winter's morning on Instagram, you might take one look at an image of this and think, "Why did I put up with that?!" Or (and I say this every year, so the message obviously isn't sinking in), "Why did I plant so many courgettes?" Now a glut of courgettes is a good way of getting to know more people in your neighbourhood. Stick a box of spare fruits by your front door with a "free" sign on top and you will soon be chatting with people and will quickly discover which of your neighbours have also grown courgettes and which haven't. (Those that have will almost certainly not be looking for more.)

If looking at images of a garden in the heady days of spring or summer is making you feel depressed about the long winter nights still ahead (perfectly natural, especially once you develop a yearning for the outdoors), turn it into something positive. This is where doing some hands-on gardening can be a great therapeutic tool for beating the winter blues. Because while you are reviewing, you can also be making a note of what you would like to do to improve the garden, and it may just be that a lot of the gardening that will help make next spring and summer extra special can be started now, despite the cold, damp, and darkness of the present day. Let's take a look at some productive things that can be done in the garden in winter—our investments for the summers of tomorrow.

Planting hope

The power of trees

Planting a tree can truly transform your garden. It is an investment in the landscape. It is creating history, setting in motion a life that in some cases could potentially outlive the one planting it. To plant a tree is to plant a landmark that can potentially serve as a host for so many wonderful things: childhood memories, nesting birds, gardeners seeking shelter or delicious edible fruits. Ok, so you might not have room in your garden for a tree that can spread into an enormous landmark, but don't underestimate the significance of planting a tree.

Think back over the significant trees from your life so far. It might sound daft, but just ponder that thought for a moment. I bet trees have played a bigger role than you think at first, even if you haven't considered yourself a gardener for very long. My mind goes back to a plum tree in my

Planting a tree is to set in motion a journey of discovery as the tree starts to ever so gradually make its mark on the landscape.

grandparents' garden and the annual event of getting the phone call that it was time to go and pick the plums. Off we would go to the tree, armed with buckets, washing-up bowls, and ladders. We would be overwhelmed with fruits most years, even though each picker helped themselves to several during the day's picking. The fun ended when one year the tree was struck by lightning. But it lives on in my memory.

Another tree that sticks in my mind is a crab apple that was outside the front door of a block of flats that I lived in years later. I didn't have a garden at the time and walking past this tree on my way to and from work each day was an important reminder of the changing seasons at a time when my connection to nature was being weakened by hours of commuting and a lack of growing space. The transition from

bareness, to blossom, to abundant small fruits smothering the ground thrilled me on a daily basis.

A dry, mild winter's day when the ground isn't frozen is a good time to plant a bare-root tree. Bare-root trees are supplied not in a pot, but with their roots bare, wrapped in a hessian sack or a plastic wrapping. Mail order tree specialists will supply trees this way and it is the best way to plant them, better than starting from trees that are in pots. Bare-root trees will have been freshly lifted from the field where they were raised and will be full of vitality and youthful vigour. Trees in pots are fine to plant, but they may have become pot-bound. This is where the roots of the trees have run out of space, so they have started to wind themselves around the pot. These

Cordons are an effective and beautiful way to plant fruit trees in a small space.

will need to be teased apart at the bottom in order for the roots to spread themselves in the soil they are planted in. Pot-bound plants will have been stressed while there was a lack of space for the roots, and this can affect how well the tree will establish.

Check how big the tree will get within 20 years before you make your selection. It must be pragmatically said that, as well as planting hope, you could also be planting a headache if there isn't enough space.

If you want to grow apple or pear trees for their fruit, you will need more than one tree in order to get a crop, because a compatible tree needs to be growing nearby to help pollinate the flowers. There may be compatible trees in the neighbourhood, but it's best to take matters into your own hands. If space is tight, you can plant varieties that bear fruits on spurs as cordons, which are decorative as well as practical and relatively easy to set up. Just plant each fruit tree with the main stem trained at a 45-degree angle to a cane and the sideshoots tied to horizontal wires.

To chop or not to chop?

When to cut the garden back

A garden doesn't have to be a barren wasteland in winter. Yes, some plants will have disappeared and naturally dropped their leaves by winter, but many can still look attractive if left intact. Robust perennial plants that have finished growing for the year can be left in the garden over winter like silhouettes, shadows of their former selves but still with an understated beauty. It is especially worth leaving these plants standing if you are in an area that gets a lot of frosts. A patch of deciduous grasses and aged structural perennials such as eryngiums, achilleas, and sedums can look simply breathtaking if captured by a crisp morning frost. It can serve as a wonderful setting for a livening 30 minutes in the garden on a winter's morning. It's a morning pick-me-up to rival the strongest coffee.

Leaving these plants intact also keeps the garden looking full over winter, and leaving old seedheads will provide valuable food for hungry birds, as well as the old plant material offering protection to any new shoots that appear unseasonably at the end of the season. It also serves as a bridge between winter and the other seasons, a reminder of how the garden looked in fall and summer. The importance of this shouldn't be underestimated, because if there is any danger of the 30-minute habit ceasing to be a way of life, it is in winter. And the danger is stronger if there is nothing at all that looks attractive in the garden.

There will come a point when it's time to cut plants back. Some will flop over in stormy weather, and if plants are flattened, then I cut them back and add them to the compost heap. Cut everything back towards the end of winter before spring bulbs are pushing through the soil. Otherwise, a tidying session can end up with lots of new bulbs getting trampled or inadvertently cut back before they have a chance to flower. This is a lesson that I have to learn time and again. My eagerness to achieve something in the garden has too often resulted in emerging plants getting flattened by my misplaced foot.

Seedheads can be stunning when left to stand in the garden through winter.

PLANTS THAT GLISTEN
ON FROSTY DAYS

Leaving structural perennials in the garden to capture the glistening frost creates a beautiful, life-affirming bridge between winter and the other seasons. Here are some plants that you will not want to deadhead or cut back.

1. *Echinacea purpurea*

Long after the petals have faded, the pompon centres of these flowers remain, looking perky framed by frost.

2. *Eryngium giganteum*

The spiky flowerheads of this drought-tolerant perennial look like the finest sculpture when edged with frost.

3. Heucheras

These low-growing perennials have curly edged leaves that look great with a crisp, frosted outline.

4. *Sedum* 'Matrona'

Keeping its summer form through winter, an established sedum covered in frost is a highlight.

5. *Stipa tenuissima*

Cascading foliage and flower stems hang beautifully in winter like frosted fountains.

An unlikely time of harvest

Reaping the rewards of summer

Winter can be a surprisingly busy season if you have a vegetable patch. Winter-hardy crops such as parsnips, leeks, chard, perpetual spinach, and winter cabbages can be kept in the ground and harvested as and when they are needed. There can also be fall-planted crops such as garlic and onions to keep an eye on. If you have some of these crops ready to harvest and tend in winter, then well done! You have truly embraced the idea of gardening being a daily way of life and not just a seasonal hobby that is picked up and dropped as quickly as a gym membership in the third week of January.

I say this because if you have crops to harvest in winter, then it is because you had the foresight to sow or plant in spring or summer, knowing that no quick results would come. You have also successfully tended them for many months to get them to winter. It's no mean feat, and one that in some ways could be likened to people who buy things in shops in July because they know they will make good Christmas presents for someone. I'm not like this at all (I leave it until the last minute before buying things), so having winter vegetables at maturity in my garden happens because gardening is part of my way of life, not because I am an ultra-organized planner, which I promise you I'm not.

The feeling of stepping outside on a cold winter's day, perhaps in the dark, clutching my mobile phone with the torch turned on, to harvest some vegetables feels more than ever like it is from another time. Perhaps I feel this way because I live on the edge of the city and would think differently if I lived in the countryside. But as many of us become more disconnected from nature, there is something comforting about engaging with the soil, donning my coat and boots (sadly, I have to admit defeat on gardening with trainers on clay soil in winter),

Rosa sericea subsp. *omeiensis* f. *pteracantha* has mighty thorns to go with its awesome name.

and harvesting crops to make a warming soup or stew. More than at any other time of year, growing plants in winter, when the rest of the world can seem shut out for such long periods, just feels like the antithesis of modernity.

The finest flowers start life as a twig

The power of planting roses

I have a soft spot for roses. I worked for a rose specialist when I was a young college student who barely knew a fuchsia from a fruit tree and became immersed in the world of these intriguing, charming, and at times infuriating but ultimately incredibly fulfilling garden plants. And for me, the fact that winter is the very best time to plant them just adds to their mystique.

Much like needing to be deliberate about sowing winter vegetables in summer, so with roses it's best to be deliberate about buying and planting them in winter when they are dormant. The ones on sale from growers will be a new, fresh crop of youngsters who will settle into the soil during the cold months before growing away strongly in spring. Roses planted from pots in spring or summer are likely to be exposed to hot, dry conditions, with a missed watering stressing the plant and hindering its development. A winter-planted rose will be more resilient. And by summer, these plants become the engine room of the garden, pumping out endless scented flowers for around four months. You can grow one in a pot if it's a big plant, along with other plants growing with it. Or squeeze one into some soil at the base of a garden wall.

Roses are best planted bare-rooted like trees, if possible, although potted roses can be planted too. Just be sure to check the plant for any old, diseased leaves hanging on and clear these away before making a purchase. These old leaves can quickly infect any new growth, which can emerge in late winter if the weather is mild.

The sight of a bare, thorny collection of twigs wrapped in a bag is probably not going to win over many people who have never grown roses before. But it's this collection of twigs that will grow and establish so much better in the garden than a plant grown in a pot and bought in flower. It is a leap of faith to buy and plant a rose in winter, but if you are just getting into the 30-minutes-a-day habit, I would strongly recommend it as a confidence builder. Remember that plants want to grow. Regardless of appearances, if you take up the challenge, you are about to add something special to the garden.

If you're still tempted to think twice about giving roses a chance, just compare them to summer-flowering herbaceous plants such as dahlias, echinaceas, and rudbeckias, and you'll realize that they are no different in having summer as their main season of interest. At least in the case of the rose, you don't have to remember where you planted it: its thorny stems will remind you—although another myth to bust about roses is that they are very thorny. Yes, some can be lethal. An encounter with the vicious winged thorns of the mightily named *Rosa sericea* subsp. *omeiensis* f. *pteracantha* will not be quickly forgotten. But many roses are nearly thornless, so pruning, training, and just walking past them doesn't have to be a hazardous experience.

When you are outdoors on a winter's day, planting a bare-root rose into brown, cold earth or putting one in a large terracotta pot on an empty patio, try to imagine midsummer and the warmth of the breeze, the hum of bees, the comfort of sitting outside in the garden in the afternoon, and the subtle, sweet scent of the roses beckoning you to come closer to them. That's why it makes perfect sense to be out here in winter, planting roses.

Being prepared

Laying foundations for plants

Winter is definitely a season of preparation, and for many old-school gardeners, winter meant one thing: digging. I vividly remember spending afternoons in winter double-digging flowerbeds when I was at horticultural college. This process involved digging a trench to a depth equal to the height of two spade blades, spreading cow manure halfway up the trench, and then digging another trench in front and covering the remaining half with this soil. We then worked our way along the flowerbed until it was all dug. Quite a performance. If you have a lot of time on your hands (and a dairy farm or stables next door), then maybe you'll want to give this a go, but it's not for me.

The no-dig method of preparing the ground in winter is a less labour-intensive technique of clearing the ground and making it more fertile, and it is arguably more beneficial for the soil. It also suits a timescale where moments in the garden are precious. My reasoning for choosing the no-dig method is more on practical grounds than scientific ones.

There are lots of benefits to not digging the soil: it helps the ground hold onto moisture, disturbs fewer weed seedlings, doesn't disturb bulbs that may be hiding beneath (something that you won't know about until spring if you've taken on a new garden), and does no damage to the structure of the soil. It also removes the need to keep checking the weather forecast,

HEALTHY ROSES TO PLANT IN WINTER

———

Whatever the space or situation, there is a rose that can take on the challenge. The best ones just keep flowering and don't present the problems with sick leaves that can put gardeners off growing them. Especially if you are new to roses, make sure to choose a variety that is particularly recommended for being healthy and disease resistant. Some older varieties are prone to disease, and it can be disheartening to watch as they develop sick leaves that start to look blemished in the height of summer. Also, look for repeat-flowering roses to ensure that you don't just get one show of flowers in summer and then no more.

I've already sung the praises of 'Princess Anne', which here joins four others of the best-performing roses, based on my experience of growing many varieties. These five have exceptional health, with lush, shiny leaves throughout the growing season. They are also all scented and will reliably flower again and again through summer and fall.

1. 'Felicia'

Charming is a word commonly used to describe roses, but it really is apt in this case. This is a great rose for nestling among other plants at the front of a patch of growing space, where its lax stems, topped with sprays of scented double, pink flowers, will gently join plants nearby, as if leaning in to have a conversation with them. I've grown this in nearly full shade, and it has still shown two flushes of flowers in summer. Height: 1.2m (4ft)

2. 'Lady of Shalott'

This is the longest-flowering rose that I have grown, starting to bloom in early summer and sometimes still showing the odd bloom at the start of winter, without seeming to take a break in-between. The scented flowers glow like a fireball, with the pointed buds showing a vivid red and yellow combination. When fully open, the flowers glow orange. It is quite a large shrub that you could train to a wall as a short climber. Height: 1.5m (5ft)

3. 'Princess Anne'

I don't know of a rose with glossier leaves than this one. The new growth in early summer looks like it has been hand-polished and is rounded with very fine teeth on the edges. The flowers are a thing of wonder as they age and show off many colours: a heady mix of red, plum, deep purple, and even a lick of yellow at the base of the petals. The flowers also have a rich scent. I'm normally quick to deadhead roses when their colour fades, but not this one. It ages so gracefully. Height: 1.2m (4ft)

4. 'Roald Dahl'

The eye-catching feature of this rose is the beautiful way that the bronzy new leaves complement the apricot flowers and dark orange flower buds. The stems are almost thornless, the flowers have a good perfume, and the plant is low and compact, forming a very sturdy subject that will keep the edge of a patio or path looking fresh and colourful for months. Height: 0.9m (3ft)

5. 'The Lady Gardener'

If you only have space for one rose and want to create a romantic, blousy, cottage garden feeling, this could be the rose you've been looking for. It has large rosette flowers (around 10cm [4in] wide) of glowing apricot that fade to white at the edges and get paler as they age. It has a nice old-fashioned scent and forms a neat shrub that is as wide as it is tall. Height: 1.2m (4ft)

hoping in vain for a day that is dry enough to dig without making a complete mess. If you have heavy clay soil in your garden, these days are few and far between. The no-dig method will help prepare the soil for spring regardless of the space, whether you just need enough cardboard from the packaging for a couple of hardback books, or you need to find someone who has just bought a giant television.

So what do you do instead of digging? Quite simply, you smother weeds using layers of wet cardboard (the rise in online shopping has made this a far more common commodity to find in plentiful supply in households than cow manure)! The cardboard is then covered with compost (up to a depth of 10cm [3in]) and allowed to slowly break down.

If you would like to do this to a large area and don't have access to enough compost, there is another possible solution, which I did in my garden. When I was digging my path, I moved all the excavated soil onto the area that was to become my vegetable patch and also threw any scraps on top, including compost leftover from plants in pots that had been moved into the garden and soil from a raised bed that I had decided to take down.

By the end of winter, I planted straight onto the soil. Granted, there were a few hard bits where I had to cut through some partly decomposed turf with a trowel, but it was far less labour than digging over the whole vegetable patch. For areas of soil that I sowed directly into, I ran the edge of a hoe along the soil to make a row. This dislodged the clods of soil or turf. Then I sprinkled a layer of compost along the row and sowed crops such as beetroot, perpetual spinach, carrots, and parsnips directly onto the compost before covering it with fine soil.

Sometimes I see skips full of soil in my neighbourhood that I guess have been removed from a garden to make way for a patio or a wall, and I always think that it must be a home that doesn't currently have a 30-minutes-a-day gardener in it. Maybe I should stop by and invite them over for a hot cup of tea.

Laying cardboard on the soil and covering it with more soil is a time-saving alternative to digging (not to mention double-digging) when you want to prepare a new flowerbed.

MORE THINGS YOU CAN DO IN
THE GARDEN IN WINTER

Protect your crops.
Cover any leafy crops such as broc-coli, cabbages, and kale with closely meshed netting to protect them from hungry birds. Kale and winter cabbages can be harvested through winter, but some, such as spring cabbages, will need to stay in the ground for a long time.

Start some sweet peas.
These beautiful, sweetly scented summer flowers are a real gift to the garden, and if sown in win-ter, they will be sturdy plants by mid-spring and in flower just before summer arrives. Sow them in deep pots and keep them in an unheated, well-lit spot indoors, or in a sheltered corner outside, away from strong winds.

Give hedges and shrubs a boost.
This is one of those jobs that is eas-ily not done, but doing it will pay off in spring and summer. Scatter a general-purpose fertilizer such as fish, blood, and bone around the base of hedging plants, flower-ing shrubs, and evergreen topiaries that are in the ground, and you'll be rewarded with strong, healthy growth in spring. If the soil is dry, water on top of the feed straight after applying it to the soil.

Check your delicate ones!
Some plants need a helping hand to stop them from being smoth-ered under the debris that win-ter can bring (perhaps a bit like humans). Check alpine plants and delicate evergreens and remove any rotting leaves that are sitting on top of the plants. It is also a good idea to spread a 5cm (2in) layer of grit around the base of alpines and evergreen shrubs in pots at this time, to ensure that water can drain away well during wet winter spells.

Put up a nesting box.
Here's a really positive thing to do in winter if you feel like life has been put on hold. Find a sheltered place on a tree trunk, wall, or side of a shed and put up a nesting box to encourage birds to come and visit the garden when they start to build nests in early spring.

5

When the lights go on

Spring

When I can feel sweat on the back of my neck
Then that's when I know it is spring
As I plant in the soil, I sow and I toil
And wonder and whistle and sing!

The beginning of
spring is the time
when you are
reminded that plants
really want to grow.

Onceyou've gotten into the groove of being a 30-minutes-a-day gardener, the start of spring will feel like the most exciting time of the year. The wonder of rebirth, of twigs becoming shrubs or fruit bushes again, bulbs bursting from nowhere to bring the brightest colours, seeds miraculously becoming little plants: it's like the arrival of old friends or a glorious reunion with family members who have been absent for a few months (well, ones you get on with, anyway).

Remember when I said that plants want to grow? This is the moment when that force of nature is as strong as ever. A green haze begins to cover even the most unpromising bare ground. Plants are growing, and it's time to embrace the changes.

Spring is a time of busyness, and the beauty of all the spring gardening tasks is that they come loaded with an atmosphere of feverish expectation. In spring, anything feels possible in the garden. Ok, so by the end of the year we might not have laid the new patio nor grown quite as much of our own produce as we had hoped. The lawn might still be a bit lumpy by fall and we might still be hopeless at remembering where we left the shed keys. But now, as another growing season begins, hope springs eternal, and it's a time to savour.

Planting identical pots and using them to line a path is a good way to make a garden seem bigger.

Channelling the exuberance of the season

Patience is a virtue

As the first signs of life emerge, there is so much that can be done in the garden. In fact, the biggest challenge for the 30-minutes-a-day gardener may be to decide what to do and what not to do. Let me explain.

I wander into a garden centre in spring and my head is turned by a vast array of vegetable and flower seeds. Row after row of colourful, promising packets of potential plants, all available for about the price of a coffee or a blueberry muffin. Surely it's too good to be true? Well, it really isn't. This is a moment when you realize that becoming a 30-minutes-a-day gardener is one of the best things that you've ever done. The miracle of nurturing crops and flowers from birth to bountiful exuberance is yours for a bit of small change in your pocket. So why isn't everyone getting on board and doing it? It's SPRING!

But why is this wonderful window of opportunity a challenge? For the simple reason that it's easy to get carried away and to decide to try and grow everything. And while this is hardly one of life's big problems, if you take on too much, the garden can get on top of you further down the line. Suddenly, those harmless-looking seedlings have turned into an army of thirsty adolescents desperate for more food and drink, and for more space where they can spread out.

Decide on what you really, really want to grow, what you want to eat from the garden, what you want to pick for a vase on your kitchen table or home office desk, and how much space you have available. Then take it from there. Sow some extras to allow for casualties—seeds that don't come up. This happens to everyone, so don't beat yourself up if some seeds don't make it: it's life. Also, sow a few extras so that you have spares to give to friends. Plants make great presents; just don't ask the recipients for progress reports each time you see them. In any case, it's great to have spare seedlings or young plants to give away to friends and spare produce to give as presents to visitors. And who knows? A few pots of home-raised plants might make friends and loved ones get that 30-minutes-a-day habit if they don't have it already.

But do think carefully before you decide what to grow in spring. If looking after young plants and seedlings starts to feel like a juggling act, then the experience of gardening can flip from relaxing to frantic. The beauty of raising your own plants in spring is that before this season is out, you'll know if you've taken too much on, and there will still be time to sow and plant more before summer arrives, or to give away some of your plants.

Pacing yourself in early spring gives you the best of both worlds. You will still have time to drink in the atmosphere of a new season of growing getting underway while also getting your hands dirty and doing your own bit to engage with the beauty and exuberance around you.

The gardening equivalent of cleaning the oven?

Mulching and early weeding in spring

To be clear, mulching plants and weeding might, for you, be absolutely nothing like cleaning the oven. But before we worry about the analogy, let's take a closer look at what's involved.

What I mean by mulching is covering the soil with a 5cm (2in) layer of compost, bark, or stones around the area at the bottom of a plant. It could be a plant in a pot on the patio, a

tree in the garden, or a cactus in a tiny container on your living room windowsill.

When it comes to raising healthy plants, mulching in early spring ticks a lot of boxes. Once in, mulch can last until fall or even the following spring. Depending on the material that you use to cover the soil, mulching can:

Mulching plants helps them get off to a good start in spring and reduces the risk of potential problems later in the year.

- block out light to prevent weed seedlings from germinating
- increase the fertility of your soil
- keep your plants' roots cool
- hold onto moisture to prevent soil from drying out
- make the base of a plant look a lot prettier

Yes, that's a pretty hefty list of benefits. But trust me: mulching can end up being an elusive task. And yes, that's why it can perhaps be a bit like cleaning the oven. The benefits are obvious, it doesn't need doing that often, and there are daily reminders that it needs to be done, but it can be difficult to get around to doing it. Maybe for you, I'm talking nonsense and the obvious analogy is (insert that thing here that's always on your to-do list).

The good news is that 30-minutes-a-day gardeners will have mastered and completed mulching by the end of spring. No doubt about it (especially after reading that list of benefits). Why? Simply because, as I mentioned at the start of the book, even people with no intention of becoming a gardener have more than likely at some point been in a garden and watered a plant, and mulching simply brings you to the next level. I guess it's like the difference between somebody who drives and someone who is a driver. Someone who drives is likely to have put windshield-washer fluid, water, or coolant into their car, but a driver has a longer list of simple but easy-to-ignore car-related duties that they find second nature to do to keep the car running as smoothly as possible.

I don't use anything decorative to mulch plants that are growing in the ground in my garden, just a good helping of compost, although the roses get an extra special health supplement: horse manure! Plants in pots and houseplants are dressed up more with a mulch of different sizes of gravel, depending on the size of the pot and the size of the plant. I use fine grit for dainty succulents and larger stones for shrubs and larger potted plants.

Knowing that the ground is well-mulched is knowing your garden is getting off to the best possible start, which is why mulching takes pride of place on your to-do list even though it's not the first thing to do in the season. Halfway through spring is the perfect time to mulch (after a good rain or a thorough watering) because the ground will be warming up and plants are actively growing. The benefits of a good spring mulch will last for months, resulting in healthier, more resilient plants.

So here we need to back up for a moment, because when plants are actively growing, so will be the weeds. Take out any unwanted invaders growing around the base of your plants as spring begins and a lot of time will be saved. Just as it will be difficult to remember that your summer tomato plants were once tiny spring seedlings, so the same can be said about the size that some weeds will become compared to those innocuous-looking little spring shoots that—like the oven—you were tempted to turn a blind eye to.

Treat plants in pots to a mulch of grit or gravel to keep roots cool and reduce weeds.

Weeds growing at the bottom of plant stems (the crown of a plant) will only get more awkward to remove later, so now's the time to put on a pair of gloves and pull them out. I used to be a firm 'no gloves' gardener, preferring to feel the soil on my fingers. I still do, but with a lot of the soil being heavy clay, I can spend those 30 minutes a day in the garden and then what feels like another 30 minutes trying to clean the soil from underneath my fingernails. I am proud of being a gardener, but not keen on making it obvious at social occasions by showing off fingernails that you could sow seeds in. I'll let people work out that I'm a gardener some way else.

It's best to pull up weeds at the base of plants by hand because trowels or purpose-made weeders may damage the roots of your plant. Now's also the time to get out any weeds that are growing in-between the plant's stems because they will probably elude you later in the year when the garden is at its fullest.

Hoeing off weeds when they are young is easier than removing large, established weeds.

Growing tomorrow's lunch

Starting edible plants

A gardening mentor of mine once told me that gardening requires sleight of hand. I don't know if you are familiar with this phrase, but I had only ever heard it in the context of conjuring tricks. When I was a kid being baffled by someone doing a card trick on the television, I was always told that it was because of the magician's sleight of hand.

So I was surprised to hear this term used in the context of gardening, although with experience, I now understand. When you start raising an army of fruit and vegetable seedlings in spring, handling delicate life forms becomes—for a few weeks anyway—a daily habit, and you learn to be as light-fingered as a conjuror in a top hat trying to guess the playing card that you have in your hand.

It is now that tomorrow's heavyweights—the colossal marrows, cucumbers, fat juicy tomatoes, and fat shiny aubergines—are like mere blades of grass being blown by the wind, and handling with care is essential. It's amazing really, when you think about it: in the excitement of spring, those hazy harvest afternoons of picking heavy crops still feel like something from another world.

The here-and-now task is to transplant a pot full of perky young seedlings into their own individual pots of fresh compost, each new home prepared with a thin tunnel for the roots to sink into.

Starting to grow vegetables and fruit from seed or buying some small plants from a nursery to nurse through their early days can seem a bit fiddly, but I find the process calming. I find listening to some music or the radio with a pot of tomato seedlings to gently separate into their own pots a therapeutic experience. It is busyness and rest all wrapped into one. I have no choice but to take my time—to be careful as I extract each new life and gently lower it into its pot, gently pushing more of the compost around the leggy seedlings with a pencil and firming it down to keep the plants upright. Then I am obliged to take more time to gently water the compost.

Evenings are spent escorting trays of young, frost-tender vegetable plants back undercover for the night, after giving them a taste of some afternoon spring sunshine.

It is a time of delicate procedures. It could be gently sieving compost to cover a tray of seeds or sprinkling tiny seeds along rows of soil outside, scraped out using the corner of a trowel,

Spring is the time
when young plants
are everywhere, and
seedlings are moved
to their own individ-
ual pots.

or later, thinning out rows of seedlings. For a time, it can feel as if everything is on a knife-edge but keep in the back of your mind the truth that nature is forgiving.

Textbooks and online searches will specify the correct sowing depth for seeds or the correct spacing for garlic cloves and onion bulbs, and this is a good place to start. But the garden will normally cut you some slack. My eldest son (aged two and a half at the time) decided to scatter some parsnip seeds over a row of strawberries in our garden in early summer. Parsnips are notoriously difficult to get to germinate, he didn't prepare the soil before sowing or follow any rules, and the last time I checked, there wasn't anyone recommending sowing parsnips on top of the nearest strawberry plants. But lo and behold, soon enough there were a few parsnip plants among the strawberries, putting up with their strange bedfellows!

This is the time to enjoy the process. Relish the moment when there are so many crops that can be started into life, and remember what we learned at the beginning: that plants *want* to grow. If they could talk, they would be cheering you on, every step of the way.

Patience is a virtue when we're nurturing youngsters

Bringing up our growing family

To be a gardener in spring is to be surrounded by youth. Maybe that's why gardeners often seem so young at heart. Young seedlings, young perennials, young shrubs, even the trees that are as old as the hills are bursting with life, covered in a green haze of succulent new shoots. This is when being in the garden for 30 minutes a day is so exciting because plants will grow noticeably overnight, with each day bringing a new

adventure. Take pictures of your plants on a Monday as the season progresses, and then take more of the same plants at the end of the week to compare them, and you won't believe how much things have changed.

I am a big advocate of buying perennial plants when they are young so that pairing them with plants that I have raised from seed and then potted individually usually gives me a fleet of plants in small pots to look after in spring. I keep them in trays so that I can move them about easily. Some, such as the French beans, tomatoes, courgettes, and half-hardy annuals, go indoors if a frost is forecast.

The main thing to be watchful for when planting out tender vegetables is slug and snail attacks. From experience, I find that there are two effective ways to keep these pests at bay. Number one is to plant out big plants. Small baby plants are far more appetizing to slugs and snails and also more at risk of being eaten past the point of no return. Number two is to mulch the plants with a layer of large stones or pebbles, spreading them around the base of the plant as far as the width of the plant.

Buying plants small and planting them when young will help them develop quickly.

Also make a shallow well around the plant, piling up the surrounding soil with a trowel. This will allow water to go directly down to the roots of the plants, rather than running off and watering weed seedlings. In turn, the plant will establish more quickly, becoming larger and better able to shrug off a pest attack.

I also protect any small plants that I bought in a garden centre that were being kept under cover. If they've been sheltered at the garden centre, it can be a shock to leave them out to the elements, even if they are plants that you know can survive the winter. Hardy pot marigolds, sweet peas, fava beans, sempervivums, and hardy perennials such as foxgloves stay outside.

The urge to plant out these plants is so strong that it is very hard to resist. But early spring is the time for the 30-minutes-a-day gardener to engage in some head-over-heart discipline. I still struggle with this, but it will pay off. If you think that frosts are gone and that your youngsters will be ok in the soil, check the weather forecast, then if you are sure, wait another week, and then do it.

The bigger that your young plants are when you plant them out, the more able they will be to shrug off a pest attack. You might have to pot up plants a few times while you wait to plant them out, re-potting into a slightly bigger pot when a plant's roots have filled its pot. And sometimes the risk of frost might be gone, but it stills pays to grow plants on in pots for longer.

Patience is always a virtue in the garden. The impetuous urge to plant out something in early spring is very strong, but trust me: by midsummer you will see no benefit of having planted a week earlier than if you had waited. And early planting runs the risk of a plant being killed by frost or damaged beyond regeneration by a slug, snail, rabbit, deer, or whatever wins the contest for your worst local pest. In contrast, the act of potting young plants into bigger ones is a therapeutic spring task—and once you've potted up, you can use any spent compost from the old pots for mulching.

Give the garden a spring health check

Especially on the patio

For me, spring is definitely a celebratory season, but I have to be honest: it's also a time for assessing the damage. Winters can be cruel, we can take chances with plants, and it is only natural that there is likely to be some collateral damage after a cold season. Whether you have mild winters or damaging ones, it is likely that you have a scenario where the extent of the winter weather is sometimes unexpected. Maybe a plant that we thought was hardy experienced a much colder winter than there had been for 10 to 15 years, and it turned out that temperatures were too low, especially for the most vulnerable: plants growing in containers. Or perhaps it was an exceptionally wet winter and some plants were overwhelmed and rotted in their pots.

Regardless of the reason, whatever you do, don't blame yourself. Sometimes we can do everything right in terms of looking after plants and find out forces of nature are much stronger than our own gardening expertise or knowledge. The winter of 2010 to 2011 in the UK took a lot of gardeners by surprise. In many areas, it was colder than it had been for years, and lots of established plants, such as cordylines, that were starting to be considered hardy (able to survive winter) here were wiped out.

Rather than despair, though, I think of events like these as a further reminder of the wonder of becoming a gardener. There is nothing boring or predictable about it. We have never truly cracked the code because we are working alongside the natural world rather than having anything like full control. We are nature's partners, learning as we go, and as we take the ride, the only thing that's certain is that nothing's certain.

Mix and match containers in spring to add extra height, detail, and color to areas of spring flowers.

And it works both ways. Sometimes extremities of climate produce a scene in the garden that is more beautiful than we ever imagined it could be: a spectacular display of fall colours or an exceptionally long summer that resulted in the taste of sweet tomatoes lingering longer than ever before. These events create memories that shape us and add poignancy and wonder amid the clutter and predictability of some elements of our everyday lives. We are poorer without them.

Being a 30-minutes-a-day gardener is as much about tuning into the richness of the natural world around us as it is about the gardening itself. So if it is a spectacular fall for leaf colour, you won't be cursing the leaves from your car window on the way to work. You will marvel at the intensity, the intricacies, and the beauty. Or, if winter is exceptionally cold, it will be an opportunity to appreciate how resilient your plants truly are rather than complain about the heating bills. Although I must confess that I still do both, I'm working on it.

So, with this in mind, spring on the patio is the time to assess how winter has left its mark. Don't feel bad about composting plants that didn't make it or those that just haven't pulled their weight. It pays to be ruthless with plants that are just hanging on, especially in pots. I see plants in containers as showpieces in my garden. They are all close to the house and viewable for most of the day, so for me there is no leeway for stragglers. If this sounds harsh, an alternative, if you have room, is to take any hangers-on out of their pots and plant them out somewhere less visible in the garden to see if they pick up, or to move them there in their containers.

I like to use the showpiece aspect of the patio to the fullest. I'm not one to insist on a tidy garden, but I see a patio as a halfway house between indoors and outdoors. So spring is the time when I clean or paint containers and wooden surfaces. I also love to mix and match, moving pots around the patio to create different combinations of colours, both through the plants and the colours of the pots themselves. Moving pots that have mixed displays of plants in them helps me to see the plants in a different light. If a plant is always growing next to the same thing, its potential as a team player could be forever hidden. That's the beauty of growing plants in pots. Switch them around to discover different combinations.

This can also be the key to improving your patio display. Move your pots around and it will probably be obvious if your container displays are missing something. Perhaps you need a tall, tropical plant in a container to add extra height and to fill in an empty corner? Or maybe some bright evergreen grasses are needed to give the patio area more fullness when the spring bulbs begin to flower.

With so much new life appearing everywhere all over the garden, spring is also a good time to clear pots of last year's rubbish. It's amazing how much debris can accumulate at the base of plants in pots, easily going unnoticed during the growing season and in winter, especially if you experience regular snowfall. Clearing, cleaning, painting, and planting on the patio in spring are among the most satisfying things that I do in the garden each year. There is a feeling of the space being both a blank canvas and a busy place at the same time. Soak up the atmosphere because it is a special time of year.

Patio potential

Assess the area, give plants in pots a boost, and be bold

I like to think of plants in pots as in temporary accommodation. Assess your patio area in spring and have a look at what you've got in pots. Maybe that lonely hebe could do with a quick burst of extra colour around it, courtesy of some miniature potted daffodils that you couldn't resist in the nursery. Or maybe that old rose that's taking up a lot of patio space would be better off planted in the ground and replaced with something taller, greener, and more dramatic? Aim to create scenes that wow you on your patio. Be bold, be adventurous, and mix and match your plants.

Shrubs, roses, trees, and fruit bushes growing in pots benefit from a pick-me-up in spring. Every two to three years, they are best taken out of their current pot and moved to a bigger one to give their roots more room. Choose a pot half again as wide and deep as the current one.

In other years, give them a boost in spring by scraping off the top 5cm (2in) of compost using a trowel. This will also remove debris, weeds, and unwanted tree seedlings that could be lurking beneath, as well as exposing any stems that might be broken. Trim these back using sharp secateurs. Replace the debris you have scraped away with a fresh layer of compost. Soil-based compost is best because it holds onto moisture well and won't dry out as quickly as general-purpose composts. If the plant is an acid-lover (a blueberry, cranberry, gaultheria, rhododendron, or skimmia, for example), use ericaceous or lime-free compost. Water the plant thoroughly and, if needed, spread a decorative mulch over the top of the compost. That's your plant set-up for the fun ahead. As a finishing touch, I like to get a damp cloth with a little bit of detergent on it and clean the outside of the pot. Use a brush to remove dried soil on the surface of the pot first.

Perennial plants can form the backbone of some splendid container displays that can add a real "wow" factor in a small space. When I had very limited growing space—most of it concreted—large pots filled with a mixture of plants with overlapping flowering times became mini, self-contained gardens in their own right. And once I had a few of them, I moved them around and joined them together to make a kind of jigsaw puzzle. I used to call it a false border. It was just a collection of maybe ten containers of mixed plants, but placed together in summer along the side of the house, it gave a flavour of the grand herbaceous borders filled with a mix of

Clockwise:

Don't be afraid to experiment with the types of plants that you put together in containers.

Evergreen plants such as *Carex oshimensis* 'Evergold' will provide year-round interest in a pot.

Carefully fill in gaps around your plants and firm the compost in well.

Spring-flowering saxifrage paired with summer-flowering osteospermum, along with evergreen grasses and succulents, will create a full-looking container display.

perennials that had always seemed so unachievable when I saw them in large gardens open to the public..

To keep the containers looking full from spring onwards, try pretty spring favourites such as saxifrages and primulas, which are useful for bringing early flowers to the edges of the container. When these have finished flowering, they can be gently teased out and replaced with some of summer's late risers, such as heleniums and rudbeckias, to give a succession of colour in the same pot. Also try mixing evergreens with spring- and summer-flowering plants in the same pot so that the season of interest is long.

Don't be afraid to experiment with the plants that you grow in containers. A key to this is keeping an open mind and not being afraid to change things that you don't like. If a plant is looking lost in a pot, crowded out by others, showing signs of stress (browning or yellowing leaves), or just not looking right with the other plants, then take it out and replace it with something else. Plants in containers will not be as deep-rooted as those growing in the ground, and if carefully teased out of the pot, planted and watered in the garden, or potted into a new pot and placed in the shade, they will soon adapt to their new home, provided that you do it before the end of spring. It's a bit risky in summer, especially in warm spells.

Plants that have completely filled their pots will benefit from being given more room for their roots to explore.

Time to experiment

Deciding what to plant in spring

As more perennial plants emerge from their winter slumber, you'll notice that some prefer a longer lie-in than others. Remember when I mentioned people who have completed a run and cooked breakfast before some of us are stumbling around, clumsily trying to make a coffee? Well, the pulmonarias, brunneras, hardy geraniums, and sedums of this world get up early, popping above the soil surface when spring bulbs are just getting into their stride. Others are heavy sleepers (I must say that I have a strong affinity with them): echinaceas, persicarias, and rudbeckias will eventually emerge through the soil as if to say, "You'd forgotten I was here, hadn't you?" It's a good idea to push stakes or large labels into the soil before these plants die down in winter, to remind you where they are. Goodness knows how many emerging perennials I have trodden on when their tiny shoots were just appearing in spring because I had forgotten that they were there! Although it's a pleasant surprise when they remind me.

The difference in the timing of when they emerge can make deciding what to plant in the garden in spring tricky. The plant stalls and nurseries will be full of early birds in spring that will scream 'impulse buy' at you, but to the uninitiated, the heavy sleepers just look like empty pots, mere compost and label. And let's be honest, it feels like a gamble to buy a pot of compost and trust that what lies beneath is the late summer–flowering superstar that you are hoping for, even if the label tells of summer colour and a plethora of flowers. Hold your nerve and trust the nursery, or buy online for delivery later in the year, but whatever you do, save some space for late-summer perennials and you will have a garden that looks colourful for longer.

Late-flowering perennials
to plant in spring

Choose perennial plants that match the type of soil that you have, and there are massive rewards to be had for such a simple task. Dig a planting hole using a spade or trowel, planting each plant at the same depth that it was in its pot. If you buy the plants as bare roots sold in a bag of compost, or if they are soilless divided plants given to you by a friend, plant so that no roots are visible but no new leaves are buried.

Make sure that the soil at the base of the hole is well broken up and not compacted. Once you've covered the roots, add some fresh compost around the base of the plant and firm the soil surface gently with the ball of your foot or a trowel to make sure that the plant is firmly planted. Thoroughly soak the plant and repeat in each dry spell through spring, summer, and early fall. The smaller the plant at the start, the less likely it is to dry out.

1. Heleniums

These are joyous plants for a slightly damp, shady spot that still receives a good few hours of sun each day. Their shades of burnt rusty oranges and reds perfectly sum up the mood of late summer and early fall. For me, they have a glorious mixture of brightness and melancholy to mark the beginning of one season and the passing of another. The flowering stems are long and thin, so these are good plants for squeezing into a gap where you haven't got room for a shrub or tree. The young shoots are prone to slug and snail attacks, so if you buy young plants in pots that have just sprouted in spring, grow them on in pots and keep them out of the way of slugs, potting them into bigger pots when their roots have filled their current homes. Then plant them out when they have made a multi-stemmed plant, which will be less appetizing to slugs and better able to shrug off an attack.

2. New England asters

These dainty little flowers come out in abundance in fall, providing such a welcome show of dreamy blooms that you will be so glad you took the trouble to plant them in spring. A lot of asters are prone to mildew, but these ones aren't and can make substantial plants if you have room. A couple of stems snipped off and put in a vase indoors will add some colour and satisfaction to your kitchen table or indoor workspace.

3. Rudbeckias

I group perennial rudbeckias (or black-eyed Susans) such as 'Goldsturm' and 'Herbstsonne' in my own category of indestructibles. They begin to flower when summer is about to bow out and they stand unmoved like colourful statues through everything that the blustery, wet, and damp fall weather can throw at them. The flowers are a vivid yellow that might prove tricky to make work with your colour schemes, but I like to pair them up with yellow roses, as well as plants that have dark foliage, such as purple-leaved heucheras, or brown grasses, such as *Uncinia rubra*. They prove a good match with the rudbeckia foliage, which is very dark green. Grow in full sun or semi shade in soil that doesn't dry out too quickly.

4. *Sedum* 'Matrona'

This plant will look like some unpromising fleshy shoots in early spring, hiding the wonder that it can bring to the garden from late summer right through until the end of winter. It will jog along unnoticed through spring and summer (but keep watering it in dry spells) then unveil flowerheads full of pretty, hot pink stars. Butterflies love these plants, and they make a great foil for late-flowering roses or mid-sized grasses, such as *Carex* 'Everest', to keep a sunny corner looking full and vibrant at the end of summer. Leave the flowerheads intact and they will look a picture when frosted. The old heads will also protect next year's shoots from cold and wet conditions when they start to emerge at the end of winter. Grow it at the edge of a path or in a pot in full sun.

Gorgeous plants to sow straight in the ground

If they don't come up, just sow some more

Do not be scared of sowing seeds directly onto the surface of the garden soil. It's not just for the super-skilful or green-fingered people. Those seeds in the packet you have in your hands want to grow as much for you as for the gardener who has being doing it for 40 years. Follow some general rules but do it with confidence; and if nothing comes up, don't beat yourself up—just sow some more!

- Check the sowing time on the seed packet. Some seeds need to be sown onto warm soil before they will germinate. Others are hardier and can tolerate being sown into cold soil.
- Mark out a row or circle with the corner of a hoe or trowel to sow the seeds in. Sprinkle compost along the surface of the row, then water the compost. This gives a nice dark surface that makes it easy to see where the seeds have landed. It also provides a free-draining surface for the seeds.
- Sow the seeds thinly along the row, then cover them with more compost. Break some compost into a sieve and shake it over the seeds to cover them. Use a cane or label to mark the area.
- Water the area where you have sown, using a watering can with a rose attachment on it, if the soil goes dusty and dry.
- Keep checking to see if seedlings have come up. In truth, this is something that you won't need anyone to tell you to do. It will become a daily habit, and a healthier one than checking for social media updates on your cellphone.

Flowers to sow direct in spring

Sowing seeds direct onto your garden soil is a great way to line a path with cheerful blooms and a cheap and easy way to fill your garden with colour in its first year—and sometimes longer—while you wait for trees and shrubs to grow up and fill their space. You can also leave seedheads to fall on the ground at the end of summer and next year's display should come up of its own accord if your soil drains well.

1. Calendulas (pot marigolds)

These bright flowers keep on going from early summer until the frosts arrive. Keep relentlessly deadheading (use snips to take off dead blooms rather than pulling them, which can uproot whole stems), then leave a few old flowerheads to scatter their beautiful curly seeds on the ground like confetti, ready for next year's display.

2. California poppies (*Eschscholzia*)

Here's a way of adding some unmissable colour to a tricky corner. These plants grow well in dry, thin, sunbaked soils, where so many plants seem to struggle. Indeed, a packet of California poppy seeds has the potential for urban regeneration. How I would love to see all those unloved, barren grass verges and empty urban planters filled with these colourful, cheerful, tough-as-old-boots flowers. If you fancy the idea of a mini wildflower meadow in your garden, mix a packet of these together with a packet of pot marigolds, sow them on the soil, and you're done.

3. Lunarias

Lunaria annua, or honesty, is named after the moon, which the round, translucent, white seed pods resemble at maturity. Lunarias have purple flowers in late spring and early summer, followed in fall by the distinctive flat, silver-dollar-sized seed pods (hence other common names including silver dollar and money plant). Seeds can be sown direct onto the soil at the start of spring, and in free-draining soil this hardy annual will seed around in following years. In fact, it has been listed as invasive in parts of the United States.

4. Nigellas (love-in-a-mist)

Among the most mysterious of garden flowers, these dainty gems have something sophisticated about them. Sow as big a patch as you can and the plants will team up to create a fluffy cloud of feathery foliage with the fringed powder-blue flowers seemingly suspended on top. It's another great choice for lining the edge of a path, ideally in full sun.

5. Nasturtiums

These plants are perhaps some of the most relentless growers that you can sow direct into the garden soil. I grow them as much for the rounded, prominently veined leaves as for the flowers. The variegated forms are unusual, with a sort of speckled frosting over them. The flowers suit a tropical planting theme in shades of yellow, orange, and red.

Still cold outside?

Plant an alpine container

Alpine plants hail from mountainous climates and many are very hardy. Most are low growing, forming cushions that are covered with flowers in spring. Start with varieties of *Saxifraga ×arendsii*, which have neat little rosettes of leaves and dainty little five-petalled flowers in many shades of pink (not to mention red, white, and purple) held just above the leaves.

Sempervivums are also easy to grow, especially for their foliage, which looks a bit like flowers in leaf-form. The foliage comes in many colours so that when lots of different sempervivums are grown together, they make a beautiful, ground-hugging tapestry.

Plant alpines at any point in spring. In the wild, they are often found growing on cliff faces, which tells us that as well as coping admirably with exposure, they also need free-draining conditions in order to thrive. Pots filled with gritty compost and topped with a grit mulch make good homes for alpines. They will also make a pretty display on the patio in spring, and if you include some attractive evergreen alpines such as sempervivums or varieties of *Sedum spathulifolium*, the containers will add a delicacy to the garden all year round.

Plant cushion-forming (low-growing) alpines slightly proud, which means that the crown of the plant is just above

Sempervivums are easy alpine plants to grow in containers.

the compost surface. Then add the grit mulch. This will help reduce the risk of the plants rotting in wet spells.

Many alpines are spring flowering, and it is almost impossible to resist putting some fresh, flowering alpines into your basket on a trip to a nursery in spring. To mix up the display in pots later in the season, try adding any taller plants that like similar conditions to create contrasts in height and flowering time. I like planting colourful osteospermums and calibrachoas with alpines in pots. These are not frost hardy so are best added at the end of spring, but they both love sun and free-draining conditions and will extend the season of interest of the alpine container until the end of summer. Just be ready to water them well during dry spells.

Discovering the art of watering

A natural rite of passage as we get in the habit

As spring proceeds towards summer, so does the need to water things. "How much water should I give a plant?" is surely one of the most asked gardening questions. I believe that this is because there isn't an exact answer. And even though the most unsatisfactory answer that can be given to a gardening advice question (or maybe any question) is "it depends," such is the reality.

There are so many variables at play when it comes to watering. What is the plant? How big is the plant? Is it growing in the ground or in a pot? How big is the pot? The reality also is that rather than be daunted by this situation, you can learn as you go. You are unlikely to kill a plant by giving it too much or too little water on one occasion.

Of course, some general guidelines are helpful. For example, if a plant is in a pot and the compost looks pale, then it is dry and the plant needs water. Another general rule is that if you pick up a plant in a pot and it feels light, then it needs water.

Sometimes there are outward signs from the plant, and for plants in the ground these will be noticeable towards the end of spring. Leaves looking a bit limp and droopy is probably a sign that the plant needs water. This is where you have to act like a detective. If the plant has drooped and the ground is dry, then these two things together will tell you that the plant needs water. If the ground is wet already, then it doesn't.

There can be a difficulty with plants not letting you know that they are thirsty at the time, then showing symptoms later. Evergreen plants are the usual culprits for this, which is why the dryness of the soil or compost at the base of the plant is a good indicator to use.

Rather than complicate matters, I'll just say this: stick to watering plants when the base of the plant is dry. Push your index finger into the soil or compost and if it is dry all the way down, then water the plant. This is essential for the good development of plants in pots and for plants in the garden that are in their first year after planting.

How much should you water? This is naturally the next question. A long drink will save you trouble compared to giving your plants a sprinkle little and often. If you water until puddles start to form on the soil surface, then this suggests that the root system of the plant will have been saturated. Just giving a little sprinkle regularly can result in a shallow-rooted plant that doesn't put down deep roots and is always drying out. A deep-rooted plant will be more resilient and better able to withstand drought conditions.

Some plants are more tolerant of dry conditions than others, but in their first year, they all need your help in producing a root system that makes them more resilient. So if you see

Knowing how much water to give plants comes with experience: the more time we spend in the garden, the easier it becomes.

a group of plants labelled as drought tolerant in a store, remember that this won't apply until they've had at least a full year in your garden. And it won't ever really apply if you grow the plant in a pot.

Still confused? There really is no better way to learn than by experience. An old boss at a garden centre where I worked when I was at college told me that if you can water well, you can do anything well, which I was slightly puzzled by. But I think that what he meant was that knowing when and how much to water comes with experience. The more you do it, the more in tune you become with a plant's needs. And the 30-minutes-a-day habit makes it much easier to get in sync with your plants.

Knowing when to water becomes difficult when we take our eyes off our plants. When we give them close, daily attention, we will become attuned to the signs that they need our help. I guess it's like looking after a friend's dog. The first time you do it you have no idea of its quirks and what's making it unhappy. After a few times you start to pick up the signs and realize why it lingers by the same cupboard (the one where the food is kept) for so long.

Missing the odd watering isn't the end of the world. Don't despair if seedlings start to droop or young plants flop over after a sunny afternoon when you didn't check up on them. Move them into shade, water them, and be amazed at the ability of young plants to bounce back in spring. You'll also find that after a full growing season of watering your own plants, you're much surer of what you are doing.

MORE THINGS YOU CAN DO IN
THE GARDEN IN SPRING

**Plant a collection of potted spring bulbs and then save
them for next year.**

You'll see these ready-made plants such as miniature daffodils and crocuses everywhere and they will instantly make your growing area seem more
welcoming. Plant them in spare gaps in containers and window boxes and
keep watering them when it's dry. After they finish flowering, lift them out
of the compost and pot them into containers that are half again as big as
the rootball of the plant. Then, while leaves are still green, keep watering
and add half a capful of general liquid plant food to your watering can each
time. This helps build up the bulb for next spring. When the leaves naturally
die down, label the pot and keep it out of the way in a shady corner until new
growth starts to sprout again at the end of next winter. Or plant them out in
a sunny spot in the garden along the edge of a path or border and follow the
same watering and feeding guidance. Label the area so you don't forget the
bulbs are there.

Lay down the lawn—do we do it?

My goodness, lawns get a lot of bad press these days. Labelled as bad for
the environment, they seem to be frowned upon in the same way as plastic straws and shopping bags. Concrete, though, gets an almost free pass in
comparison. A lot of this lawn-bashing seems to be based on the presump-
tion that you need a petrol- or electric-powered mower to look after them,
and that you need to keep them as short as a tennis court. Neither is true. A
manual cylinder push-mower will cut your lawn cleanly without your having
to regularly fill it with fossil fuel or connect it to a power supply, and it makes
very little noise compared to the drone of an internal combustion engine.
Just mow little and often because push-mowers can struggle to cut thick,
long grass.

Obviously, if your lawn is large this isn't practical. For large lawns, keeping the grass reasonably long will make it less likely to turn brown in dry spells and reduce the amount of time that you have to spend mowing. If the lawn doesn't come in for constant use as a kids' sports field, then keeping a lot of it long and mowing shapes or paths into it will encourage a lot of wildlife and make it a fun feature. You'll be surprised at the wildflowers that can emerge and, as with so much of nature's finery, they are likely to conjure up a scene that would be difficult to deliberately plant.

Spring is a good time to make a new lawn—sow seed onto damp, level ground after a good rain, and leave it uncovered. Or lay some turf if your budget allows. It's also the perfect time to lay wildflower turf, which will fast-forward the process of creating a meadow in your garden and is ideal for creating a little pocket of ground that will attract lots of beneficial insects to the garden. Turf will need a lot of watering, while lawns from seed will only need watering pre-germination unless you go a week without rain. A lawn sown from seed can transform bare ground from brown to green in a matter of weeks and be ready for a first mow six weeks after sowing in spring.

Chop back hard.
It's not as scary as it seems!

Cutting back plants hard (cutting away most of the plant) can be a scary thing to do, can't it? Especially if you're just getting into that 30-minutes-a-day habit. Confidence is key, and the more you prune, the less fear will be involved with it. The thing to remember is that pruning is a positive thing to do to a plant. It's like when we get a haircut (unless you don't think of this as a positive thing).

There are a few plants that benefit from being cut back very hard in early spring. Buddleias, cornus, hardy fuchsias, and ornamental grasses that have started to produce spring shoots can all be chopped back to near ground level. This sounds like a terrific gamble, right? Well, the truth is that you'll never look back. It will make way for lots of healthy new growth that will bear this year's flowers without the baggage of last year's old, tired material holding it back. I guess it's a bit like putting your fall and winter woolly clothes back in the wardrobe and getting out your lighter spring ones. For these plants, cut back each stem to 15cm (6in) above ground level. Use clean, sharp tools so that you make clean cuts and then wait for the plant to respond with fresh, healthy growth that will result in no fear next time around.

Plant summer-flowering bulbs.
Here's a garden-boosting task that is so easily forgotten amid the frenzy of activity in spring. The time to plant summer-flowering bulbs is towards the end of spring when the soil is warming up and the risk of very cold temperatures has passed.

These are some of the garden's most bold and showy flowers, although white forms will work well if you're looking for a more subdued, understated look in your garden. We're talking dahlias, gladioli, lilies, begonias, crocosmias, and freesias. This is also the time when you are most likely juggling lots of sowing, moving plants indoors and outdoors to acclimatize them, and planting and nurturing seedlings. The good thing is that it's not a long-winded task:

- Find a sunny part of the garden or some empty pots—at least 30cm (12in) wide—and you've got a home for summer bulbs.

- Use a fork to dig over the planting area to relieve it of any compacted soil.

- Dig planting holes that are twice as deep as the height of the bulb.

- Add a good handful of multi-purpose compost mixed with grit into each planting hole before you fill it with soil

- If you can't tell which way up to plant a bulb, plant it on its side and it will naturally right itself.

- Water well after planting and push large labels or canes into the soil to mark the area where you have planted—it's so easy to forget.

Previous, clockwise:

Sowing is the most practical and cost-effective way to start off a good-sized area of lawn.

Tread over the ground to create a level surface for sowing a new lawn.

Cornus (dogwood) can be cut back to just above ground level to encourage vibrant new stems to grow.

6

Why we
do it

Summer

Living life in the fast lane
And the slow lane
At the same time
Bliss

Summer is a time of
fullness, bright colors,
and endless flowers,
but take time to step
back and enjoy the
moment.

As spring turns to summer there is a wonderful moment in the garden when each plant presents itself full of poise, at a youthful peak. There may be more flowers later, stronger growth still to come, and more fruits and roots to harvest in the weeks and months ahead. But now, for a brief few weeks early in the season, grace and elegance are everywhere, posing for the camera.

There is also much more than the eye can see: the sounds, the scents, a softness in the air. Sunny days are long, and 30 minutes doesn't feel like nearly enough time to be out in the garden. A lot is happening: seeds germinating, popping their heads through the surface of the soil; seedlings on windowsills stretching towards the light; shrubs covered in soft new leaves and fresh flowers; rose bushes bursting into beautiful scented blossom. Then there's the excitement of the first pickings of the crops sown in spring: salad leaves, radishes, early potatoes, and the first strawberries. For some of us, eating the first strawberry is when summer officially begins.

Summer is as full of hope and expectation as spring—as the season progresses, so much will come to fruition. Plants will grow and the garden will develop at a pace that renders last week as ancient history. Go away from the garden for a few days and you almost won't recognize some of your plants when you return. It's a bit like not seeing a friend for a while and then struggling to recognize them when you meet up because they've let their hair grow.

At such a frenetic time, the 30-minutes-a-day habit will help you stay on top of the growth of weeds and the plants that you want to grow. Both can easily be controlled (as much

With so much to see in the garden in summer, take time to witness the explosion of flowers and bright colour.

as you deem necessary) when you have the daily habit. But as well as being industrious during the day, we need to take time to be still in the garden and to "face north" if we want to take in everything that's happening and make the most of the lighter evenings. A daily garden habit allows summer to be a season of both busy activity and quality time to rest and reflect, and for this it is worth its weight in gold. No expensive holiday or micro-managed social event can conjure up a feeling equal to that of knowing that you belong in the garden in summer, whether at work, at rest, or at play.

A note on micro-management: summer is a season when expectations can be high for what can be achieved in the garden, but don't be too hard on yourself if you don't complete as many projects or harvest as much home-grown produce as you had hoped. Just take every opportunity to be in the garden, soak up the atmosphere, and enjoy this amazing space for what it is, rather than fretting about what it could be. Once you've got the daily habit, the garden will naturally evolve and develop. It's possible to work and work and work in the garden and never find any contentment in it.

Take time to "face north" as the sun sets on warm evenings, to relax in a chair with a good book and some good company (sometimes that equals being with friends, sometimes being by myself). I had to learn to do this the first summer in our garden when there was far more rubble, rubbish, and bare soil than I would have liked and the phrase *work in progress* was an understatement. But it was a beautiful place to be on a summer's evening, just taking a few deep breaths and observing the sights and sounds. Keep facing north in summer and you'll find that the garden as a whole is worth far more than the sum of its parts, even if it's partly a building site.

Leaves of beetroot
seedlings sacrificed
to make more space
for roots to develop
can be used fresh in
a salad.

Early summer help for seedlings

Thinning and staking

So we've spent all this time waiting for seeds to grow. Maybe we sowed in hope rather than expectation, before becoming a little over-excited when that miraculous row of tiny shoots popped their heads above the soil. So why am I about to tell you that the next thing to do is to rip a lot of these seedlings from the soil completely—this sounds a bit brutal, doesn't it? I have heard gardeners say that they have to pot on every single tomato seedling that germinates, even if it means having more tomato plants than they have room for, because they can't bear for any to end up binned or composted. And in the same way, it can seem strange to pull up precious growth that you waited weeks to see.

Yet thinning out is the key to bigger crops in many cases. No matter how sparsely you sow seed direct into the soil in a row, there will be seedlings that should be sacrificed to allow others more room to grow. You have to be cruel to be kind. Those seedlings of radishes, carrots, spinach, and beetroot will need space in order to come to fruition.

Rows of seedlings for root crops need thinning to every 10cm (4in) unless you want to harvest them as baby vegetables, in which case every 5cm (2in) will be fine. The bonus with spinach, beetroot, Swiss chard, and lettuce is that the thinnings can be washed and thrown into a salad—not every thinned-out seedling will be extinguished in vain.

A slightly sticky situation with thinning out is carrots. Thinning out the seedlings can release a scent that alerts carrot root flies who then proceed to tunnel into the roots and make the crops more or less useless. I've dug up rows of carrots that resemble flutes rather than solid root crops because carrot flies had got into them. Maybe I should have tried to get a tune out of them!

I've also experimented with not thinning out carrots, letting all the young plants stay crammed in like passengers packed into a train car. I ended up with an almost comical collection of knobbly roots, a few of them actually resembling carrots. They all tasted fine, but I seemed to lose hours of my life trying to peel them, narrowly avoiding injury on a few occasions. These quibbles aside, the roots were small and thin, and the yield was such that I couldn't help thinking that I might have been better off leaving the row bare to grow wild and attract a few bees instead.

A more satisfying way around the carrot conundrum, though, is simply to sow the seed as thinly as possible so that all the young plants aren't jostling for position with each other.

Staking is a quick job that is best done in early summer— if you didn't have time in spring—when so many perennial plants are full of that poise, grace, and elegance that I mentioned earlier. These can soon be lost if plants are not staked and a windy spell of weather arrives when growth is soft and easily spoiled. Push purpose-made plant supports or hoops of wire over young perennials in early summer and you should still end up with a natural-looking display. If you've got a block of perennials growing near each other that could all do with some support, you can also insert a series of short canes into the soil at regular intervals and wind string around them, then tie it securely, to make one big support for everything.

Peas need support to give you the best crop possible.

Staking a plant after it has been damaged by wind is a bit like shutting the stable door after the horse has bolted: plants can look awkward and unnatural. If they are damaged in early summer, it's far better to cut them back, then stake them when early regrowth begins.

Peas also need staking, to keep their leaves above the ground and to prevent the pods spoiling from being in contact with the soil. Push tree prunings into the soil at angles along the row to support them.

Creating the perfect patio

Cultivate a place to be

Patios are special places in the garden. Sometimes they are the only places. It's been the case for me, when my garden was just a tiny concrete strip with only a couple of small spaces of exposed soil. Why are they special? For me, a patio acts as an extension of indoors, a place to sit, talk, have parties, catch up with a friend over coffee, or escape from everyone and everywhere else, with a good book or just your own company. It is a place where life has its own heartbeat compared to the inanimate nature of indoors in which even the most lovingly tended houseplants fail to create the same vibe as outdoors (for me, anyway, and I've got a lot of plants indoors).

I say this despite having lived only in places with a temperate climate. Sadly, summers in the United Kingdom are rarely made up of week after week of predictably warm, sunny weather. And so it can be difficult to get in the habit of truly living outdoors in terms of eating, socializing, or having quiet time to yourself. Barbeques here are best organized on the day rather than weeks in advance, unless everyone is comfortable with bringing a sweater and an umbrella. But the 30-minutes-a-day habit will make it more likely that you will want to seize every opportunity to get out in the garden.

Enjoying the patio in summer will often spark new ideas, sometimes for practical reasons. Maybe your regular favourite place to sit is just a bit too draughty, and a windbreak plant such as a black bamboo or a large fatsia will provide some shelter and give off a warmer, tropical vibe. Or perhaps you think the place needs an extra splash of colour, and you decide to give some containers or garden furniture a fresh coat of paint. For me, a patio is a place of both passivity and creativity. I will break up my garden time to sit, soak up the sun, and relax in the middle of a summer's day when I get the chance and the weather is

In summer, a patio is an extension of the indoors and plants in containers will help create an enticing atmosphere.

kind, then embark on another mini-project in the welcome coolness of the evening as the sun goes down.

I know that some people consider a patio to be a place of toil. The thought of growing plants in pots conjures up thoughts of having to spend hours watering, but container growing is not always more labour-intensive than growing plants in the ground. In terms of how much time you have to spend maintaining plants, there are reasons why both container and garden growing can save time and add time. Some plants in pots may need a lot of water in summer, but they may need less pruning or weeding than those in the ground, and they are easier to contain and prevent from spreading into the territory of others. Regardless of the time each pot may take up, once you have the 30-minutes-a-day mentality, it won't even matter if some plants need regular attention, In fact, you will probably end up a bit disappointed if they don't. One-way relationships never seem to end very well.

Patio revamp

Summer is when it becomes obvious if the patio could do with being bigger, smaller, less crowded, cleaner, or otherwise different. As you start to live in the garden in summer, it's easier to work out how improvements can be made, the same as for rooms indoors. There are some easy ways to improve a patio without having to re-lay the whole lot. Removing a paving slab from the middle of a patio can help to soften the space by creating the ideal place for a living feature such as an upright evergreen tree, for a Mediterranean vibe, or a summer-flowering shrub to add some special flowers or scent to the area while you relax there in summer. Scraping out loose mortar from the joins between the slabs and refilling them with a fresh, slightly damp mix of four parts sand to one part cement mixed with water will smarten the patio and will also remove weeds and maybe moss along the way.

Scented rose 'Vanessa Bell' grows well in containers and makes a beautiful feature for the patio in summer.

So how do we go about creating that dream patio? It's all a case of priorities. Start living in your patio area. Sit down in it whenever you can on several different half-hour stints in the garden and you'll soon find the part that's most comfortable to you, even if it makes no sense to anyone else. Or perhaps it doesn't click there and you need to find your space or create shelter somewhere else in the garden.

Also prioritize what you want to do in the area. Is it crying out for a chiminea for toasting marshmallows and keeping guests warm as you sit out under the stars? Or does it need a large fire pit if more room is available?

Then think about plants. Are there plants that you love but that aren't suited to your garden soil? Maybe you would love to grow blueberries, rhododendrons, or cranberries, but you haven't got the acidic soil that they crave? Pot growing is the answer. Or maybe there are plants that you like so much, you would like to be able to see them more often by growing them on the patio, close to the house and maybe visible from indoors? And don't forget the dimension that scented plants can bring to the patio. Scents are such powerful things in the garden. They provide a tantalizing link to the past as much as sweetening the present. A scented-leaved pelargonium in a pot on a patio table instantly transports me back to my grandparents' conservatory windowsill.

Why we do it

If the patio becomes a place where you want to be at night, then lighting is a key consideration too. An outside power socket makes it easy, as do battery-powered lights that can be easily brought indoors to keep them dry. Or even just having a security light fitted above your back door can be sufficient to light up a small patio enough to make sitting outside in comfort possible.

Creative planting with succulents

Succulents are the perfect plants to add to the garden in summer. They love being baked and exposed to full sun and, after an initial long drink, they can just be left to get on with it. Lots of them are hardy too, so it's not a temporary fix, provided they are grown where the soil drains very well. Even ones that need protection in winter (such as a lot of echeveria varieties) can be brought indoors onto a well-lit windowsill in mid-fall, before the lingering, damp mornings and evenings kick in.

If you see a gap between paving slabs or in walls, try a trailing sedum or a hardy sempervivum. They don't need much in the way of soil; a 50:50 mix of soil and grit will be fine to plant them in. If you have mixed containers of plants that don't need boggy conditions, pop a succulent in to add a quirky feature. Also try pairing succulents with other drought-tolerant plants that perhaps aren't known as natural bedfellows. Try them in a pot with Mediterranean herbs or with sun-loving, drought-resistant calibrachoas, which will flower almost nonstop all summer.

Therapy in that comfortable place

Relaxing and doing at the same time

Opposite, top to bottom:

Patio growing allows you to grow plants that may not be suited to your garden soil—here a 'Coral Reef' sedum shares space with a deep orange calibrachoa.

Succulent plants such as this 'Angelina' sedum grow well alongside drought-tolerant osteospermums, hebes, and calibrachoas in a mixed container.

Summer could well be the season when it dawns on you that you have become a 30-minutes-a-day gardener. It's a sunny summer's afternoon, perfect for relaxing in the garden—and you find yourself doing exactly that. Except that you're not relaxing by putting your feet up and imagining that you are on a beach somewhere hot and exotic. Instead, you're quietly snipping away the dead flowers of a bushy marguerite, or clipping a slightly untidy-looking evergreen hedge. Or snapping the spent blooms of a favourite rose to allow more memorable blooms to follow. The moment when it dawns on you? It's when you do these things without thinking, and enjoy every second of it.

Perhaps deadheading is the ultimate form of summer relaxation in the garden. It's the gentlest, simplest garden task, one that can be done with the kids (especially if you are prepared for a few mishaps), and one that goes a long way towards keeping the garden looking colourful all summer. A pair of sharp snips is my preferred tool for deadheading (small scissors for kids). Secateurs or pruners are fine too, but the lighter the tool the better if you've got a lot of snipping to do—it will take the strain away. If I'm in a rush or just popping into the garden very quickly, I almost instinctively think it's a good idea to pull a few old flowers off plants as I'm walking past, but I've tried to stop doing this. The thing with deadheading by hand is that if you start pulling on an old flower stem, you can end up pulling up quite a lot of the plant itself by accident. This is especially likely with plants that have long flower stalks such as pot marigolds and perennial wallflowers and when kids are helping.

Removing spent flowers in summer is an easy, rewarding task that encourages more fresh flowers.

Opposite: The cheerful flowers of marguerites (*Argyranthemum*) will be a presence all summer long if you keep deadheading.

I'm not an obsessively neat gardener, but when it comes to deadheading, I seem to find a desire to be tidy. A neatly deadheaded plant in summer, with all its flower stems trimmed back to the nearest pair of leaves, is like someone who has left the house with their A-game on: clean, well-dressed, hair on point, on top of the world. For me, summer is when so many plants can look a million dollars and I feel a desire to preen them so that they look at their best. If old flowers are just

snapped off the top of their stems by hand, you'll also be left with a lot of snags of old stem that will just die back and go brown. And snipping back the flower stems gives you a chance to shorten any plants growing in a lop-sided fashion. None of these things would bother me as much once we hit the middle of fall. The season feels different then. But in midsummer, the garden is in the prime of life, so why wouldn't it want to look as sharp as possible?

If this all sounds too painstaking and you can't ever see yourself becoming a tidy gardener, then fair enough, do your thing. If you have many dead flowers to remove, then you can save a lot of time by using a pair of sharp shears. If you don't mind sacrificing a few new flower buds, lightly shear over the top of perennial wallflowers, marguerites, or perennial salvias, and all the old stems can be gone in a couple of cuts. You will lose a few new buds, but the plants will soon bounce back, and if you make cuts just below a pair of leaves, you'll end up with bushier, stockier plants too.

Forgiving yourself

When things haven't turned out as planned

This could be the most important thing that you do to get the 30-minutes-a-day habit locked in: be able to forgive yourself. By the time that summer has arrived, there could well be signs that some things have gone wrong. But relax. This is life! Sometimes things don't go according to plan, but it doesn't matter. Some seeds mysteriously never appear above the soil surface. Maybe it was too cold or too dry at just the wrong time. Maybe mice ate the seeds. Or perhaps it was a bad batch of old seed that never would have germinated anyway.

It's good to be nimble as a gardener and to keep creating new opportunities for hope and new life. Rather than conduct a prolonged post-mortem or beat yourself up and say that you'll never have green fingers, just have another go! Sow new batches, plant new crops, replace a plant that failed with something new. A garden is in a constant state of regeneration and cycles of life, all the more so if we stay proactive and don't dwell on something that didn't work.

Now of course it's good to find out why things go wrong and to try and avoid the same thing happening again. If flea beetle peppered all your young salad seedlings with little holes, spraying a new batch with water every evening should solve the problem. Or if early-sown carrots didn't come up, try a few weeks later when the soil is warmer. If direct-sown seeds are consistently failing to appear, try sowing them direct on a 5cm (2in) deep row of damp, good-quality compost (then cover them with additional compost) just before rain is forecast.

If slugs destroyed all your young vegetable plants, sow some more and grow them on to twice the size of the others before you plant them out. Or sow them direct at the start of summer and cover them with a cut-off plastic bottle to keep them safe until they are big and able to shrug off a slug attack. Remember that well-worn phrase I keep using, that plants want to grow? When the gardener refuses to be beaten and wants them to grow too, then the sky is the limit.

Trusting nature's pace

Making the most of the conditions

No matter how slow you decide to take life in the height of summer, the garden moves fast. Grass grows fast, crops grow fast, weeds grow fast. To the uninitiated this is a big problem. (Remember that frenzy of garden blitzing that I mentioned earlier?) But midsummer also offers a massive opportunity. While it may feel like everything is growing up too fast, like a child that becomes a teenager too soon, the garden is actually cutting you a lot of slack. Courgette seeds sown direct into the soil in early summer will soon replace any spring-sown young plants that were gobbled up by slugs. It's the same for French and runner beans. Ok, so the pea crop sown at the start of summer wasn't a great success. No matter, there's time to start another from scratch. Or maybe a rose bush has gone berserk by the middle of summer and is swamping other plants. No worries, you can cut back all the gangly stems and you'll still get more flowers later. So many crops can still be sown in midsummer, yet it's easy to take these opportunities for granted and miss the boat. You can get to the end of summer and wonder why you didn't sow more batches of salad, more replacement plants, more sunflowers, more of your newest crush.

I wonder if a stumbling block in summer is that it is so easy to get fixated on weed control and keeping the garden tidy, and forget that new life can be added to the garden all through the season. In summer it's so easy—and understandable—to get tunnel vision in the garden and only have eyes for the things that take our attention in the here and now. Those tomatoes that have been nurtured from seed since March or potatoes planted on a biting cold day in early April become like our offspring. Having the foresight to begin more crops while we lavish attention on the ones that we have lovingly raised for months can be difficult.

Leave areas for wildlife

Leaving patches of the garden to go wild is likely to greatly encourage insects and birds to visit the garden and you may see some wildflowers popping up too. It will encourage a healthy ecosystem, so pests are less likely to be a problem. The easiest way to do this is to let some of your lawn get long and see what happens, or leave a corner of the garden wild, adding a pile of old logs and some bird boxes. If space is tight, you could tightly pack a pot with bamboo canes cut to the height of the pot, turned on its side and placed in a sunny, sheltered corner. This should be an ideal nesting site for bees.

A log pile will encourage insects into the garden and can make an attractive feature too.

Set yourself weekly reminders on your calendar or your phone to sow something new. In early summer move a table and chair to a warm part of the garden and make it your "sowing" corner. From there, figure out where to plant some fall-flowering bulbs. Sit back on a summer's evening, sow some seeds, pour a long drink of something cool and refreshing, and, as the poem says, live life in the fast lane and the slow lane. Soaking up the atmosphere of summer takes on a new dimension when we are actively engaging in the powerful potential of the season, a season that can cause seeds and bulbs to rapidly burst forth, grow, and produce a timely harvest as much as it can cause pale skin to get frazzled by sun and the lawn to grow noticeably overnight.

Fall-flowering bulbs
to plant in summer

New life can be added to the garden all through the summer. Here are some special bulbs for fall interest.

1. *Crocus speciosus*
The exquisite pale blue flowers appear before the leaves, creating an unusual display that adds interest in a gravelled area. Prefers full sun and gritty, unimproved soil. Height: 10cm (4in)

2. *Cyclamen hederifolium*
A dainty plant that looks lovely coating the ground underneath a tree in fall, creating an effective, near ground-level display that evokes a feeling of spring. It is perfect for shade or part shade. Height: 10cm (4in)

3. *Gladiolus murielae*
A graceful flower with gently arching stems showing off scented pure white flowers with a deep purple throat. Grow in well-drained soil.

The bulbs need digging up after leaves have died down and storing indoors until planting again next summer. Height: 10cm (4in)

4. *Nerine bowdenii*
Grow this unmissable, high-impact, electric pink bulb in a sheltered, warm, very well-drained spot in soil that has not had compost or manure added to it recently. Height: 45cm (18in)

5. *Sternbergia lutea*
Rich yellow goblet-shaped flowers will light up the patio if you plant a pot full of these bulbs in late summer. The leaves are slender like grass, allowing the flowers to be shown off fully. Grow in any well-drained soil or good-quality potting compost. Height: 15cm (6in)

Filling in the gaps

When the garden starts to come together

I'm sure you're familiar with the plant centre trolley dash.
You know the drill. Spring slowly turns to summer. You have
a weekend free or a day off, and something in the warm air
draws you towards the nearest place selling plants. This seems
to happen to a lot of people all of a sudden at this time of
year, whether they are into gardening or not. Thirty minutes
is easily lost shopping for plants. And this can be the start
of people deciding that gardening isn't for them, if they fill a
trolley full of colourful plants and then a few weeks down the
road they have nothing to show for it. It's easily done. Buying
plants that are in flower is a perilous business. Some will stop
flowering in a couple of weeks and not start again until the
following spring. Others may have been forced into flower arti-
ficially and sulked after being exposed to lower temperatures
outdoors.

The more we get to know our garden, the less likely this is
to happen to us. For sure, there's no substitute for taking the
time to look up the names of plants, their flowering times, and
their season of interest. Taking your phone along with you and
looking up the plants as you see them can save a lot of disappointment. But as the garden becomes a meaningful part of
our lives, the urge to grab the latest splash of colour is likely to
be replaced by more nuanced, longer-term thinking. A bit like
my earlier example of how planting becomes weeding with a
new garden, as ground starts to get cleared so new things can
be planted, a similar thing will happen in summer. Gaps in
the garden or areas that can be joined up will become more
obvious than in winter and spring, when gaps are only to be
expected while so many plants lie dormant.

In summer the gaps are noticeable and filling them is great fun. Summer planting doesn't get recommended in many textbooks but I find this strange. The thinking behind it is that the plants can easily become stressed if planted at a time when it is more likely to be hot and dry. Yet this doesn't stop us planting many hungry and thirsty vegetable crops and it shouldn't stop us planting other things either, although we will need to play close attention for the immediate month or so after planting. The 30-minutes-a-day habit means that there is ample opportunity for any problems to be pre-empted. Inspect the garden each morning or evening and watering needs can be addressed or unmulched plants identified and sorted out. Plant in the evening, water very well, spread a mulch, and check the newly planted plants every day or two for the first couple of months. Regularly check after that and remove any weeds around the base of the plant. Feed plants that are summer flowering with a high potassium liquid plant food every couple of weeks. And that's it.

As you spend more time in the garden and your vision for the place grows, what to fill gaps with is less likely to be based on the first thing that you notice at the plant centre. You may also have trays of young annual plants all ready to be planted out. And as your appreciation for plants

Feeding plants

While established trees and shrubs don't really need feeding in summer, some plants are hungrier than others. Annuals in pots such as calibrachoa, nemesia, and annual salvias will give many more flowers if regularly fed. To get in the habit of feeding, add one quarter of the recommended dose of a high-potassium liquid plant food each time you water in summer. Summer-fruiting crops, including peppers, beans, tomatoes, chillies, courgettes, and cucumbers, need regular food and can be fed in the same way as annual plants. Roses in the ground will give a good show if fed twice, once at the beginning of spring and then again at the start of summer. Sprinkle a granular rose fertilizer at the base of the plant and water in well. Feed roses in pots as you would annuals.

Late summer-flowering plants such as *Coreopsis grandiflora* 'Presto' are perfect for filling gaps in a sunny position.

grows, take the time to seek out plants that aren't in flower. If
they look fresh, healthy, and full of growth, then there's a good
chance that they are primed to flower later in the year to bring
extra colour to the garden.

Starting to gather a harvest

The joy of results

You will probably feel as if the sky is the limit when you harvest that first crop or pick that first bunch of flowers, grown
from seed, to place on your desk indoors. The first little vic-
tory of summer is something to relish. And while you may be
overwhelmed by those impossibly good pictures showing up
on Instagram, remember that what you see on social media
is not necessarily what it seems. Instead of comparing your
garden to what you see on your phone, celebrate your own
moments of joy that tell you summer is here along with the
miracles that come with it: beautiful flowers or sweet fruits
that have been harvested from your garden.

Don't despair if your recently planted fruit trees or bushes
bear no fruits or only a handful. They will take two or three
growing seasons to hit their stride and produce a heavy
crop. This is true of all your soft fruit, from strawberries and
raspberries to blueberries and gooseberries. But you should
notice an incremental increase in the amount of fruit that
you harvest each year, especially if you cover the plants with a
finely meshed netting to keep birds from helping themselves.
This will be less of a problem once your shrubs and trees are
mature and there will be enough to go around for everybody.

Why we do it

171

Embracing the warmth

Getting the most from plants in hot weather

Although (if you're like me) you may spend large parts of the year longing for warmer weather, there does come a point at which heat in the garden can be more of a threat to some plants than an advantage. Plants with thin foliage and soft stems such as rudbeckias and young fuchsias will be at the mercy of hot sun and high temperatures.

Plants that have been in the garden for two years or more will be able to cope better than those planted in the same year, which could need daily attention at times. If the plants are in pots, the easiest thing to do (so long as the pots are not too heavy) is to move them into shade during the hottest part of the day. Planting pots with a mixture of equal parts soil-based compost and multi-purpose compost will help keep them light and easily manoeuvrable.

Water plants newly planted in pots as often as every morning or evening in hot summer spells. Placing a saucer under each pot will help catch water that escapes through the drainage holes. However, if you have a rodent problem, empty the water straight back onto the plant five minutes later or your four-legged friends will think that you've put out a drinking station for them.

Spreading a gravel mulch over the compost surface will help keep plant roots cool as well as making pot displays look neater, but bear in mind that when the compost is covered by grit, it can dry out without this being obvious, at least at first. Do a test watering and see how quickly the plant takes up the water in the saucer. If it goes fast, then you know that the plant is very dry.

Fuchsias in pots are best moved into a shady position in very hot conditions.

As days start to get warmer, make the most of being able to sit out and enjoy relaxing in the garden. It's such a special time of year, but it will go by in the blink of an eye if you spend it in a frenzy of busy-ness. In the season ahead there will be ample opportunity for this. For now, though, the sights and sounds of the garden at the end of spring have a different feel, one of freshness and promise.

MORE THINGS YOU CAN DO IN THE GARDEN IN SUMMER

Plant fall-flowering bulbs.
If it's easy to forget to plant spring-flowering bulbs in fall, then remembering to plant fall-flowering bulbs in summer is a sure sign that you are becoming a gardener. Fall crocuses, nerines, and sternbergias are lovely choices. If space is hard to come by, or if you don't trust yourself not to walk all over them, grow the bulbs in containers filled with three parts multi-purpose medium to one part bulb-planting compost, and mix a good handful of grit into each pot. Water them, and keep the pots in a semi-shaded spot through the rest of summer. Label them well so you don't mistake them for empty containers at some point in the near future.

Decide on your pest strategy.
This will potentially be a big time- and money-saver. The easiest way to not let pests bother you in the garden is to learn to live with them. Concentrate your energy on keeping your plants growing healthily and they will be more likely to shrug off pests. Plant out vegetable plants as late as possible (when they are as big as possible) and slugs are less likely to be a problem. Just flick or wipe aphids off the stems of your roses and they are unlikely to do much harm. Use your daily stroll through the garden to keep an eye out for caterpillars on vegetables so you can pick them off when they are tiny. Yes, you could spend hours taking on a spraying, pest-control mission, but in my experience it

Use scissors to harvest some succulent young peashoots—they will transform a salad.

Far right: Runner beans mature so fast in summer that it is best to check them every day and pick them before the pods become swollen and dark green.

just turns the garden into a battle-ground where every day becomes a fight, and the desire to keep return-ing to it will wane over time.

Pick fast-maturing crops.
Keep on top of harvesting cut-and-come-again salad leaves, and remember that you can sow new batches at virtually any time. Harvest them when they are the size you want them. Also check peas and beans daily to see if they are ready for harvest. Peas are ready when the pods are fat but still shiny, and you may also want to harvest the tasty young leaves. If the colour is draining from the pods then they are losing their freshness. Runner beans will also need daily picking. Pick them when the pods have fully formed—you will be able to easily tell which of the narrow-shaped youngsters aren't ready—but haven't turned dark or fat.

Feed spring bulbs.
For a colourful display next spring, bulbs that have finished flower-ing benefit from being given a high-potassium liquid fertilizer for six weeks to help build up their reserves. If the bulbs are growing in thick grass, carefully mow as much grass from around the bulbs as you can, so that the plant food can get right down to the roots of the bulb. Feed weekly for six weeks after flowering and leave the foliage intact, allow-ing it to die down naturally.

Give your houseplants a vacation.
Gradually acclimatize some of your houseplants to outdoor conditions and your patio or outdoor seat-ing area will feel even more like a home. Wait until there is no risk of frost, then place them in a shady spot for a couple of weeks, bring-ing them indoors at night. Then they will be ready to warm up your outdoor space until the middle of fall. Keeping them outside will blow the cobwebs off your houseplants, dispersing dust and showering them with precious rainwater to drink, which they much prefer to tap water. With the exception of cacti and succulents, your houseplants will need regular watering each time the compost goes dry.

A sheltered place on the patio is a great place to show off your houseplants in summer.

7

The end and the start of the party

Fall

Older
But more intriguing
Slower
But still standing
We fade, we glow, we wither, we grow
And life moves on

The garden takes on
a new richness and
fullness as summer
turns to fall.

In another world, fall would be the start of the gardening year: time to plant bulbs, sow seeds that need a winter dormancy, and lift and divide perennials that have grown too big. It's a time when a lot of new things can be set in motion. Yet the start of fall can pass by unnoticed, even if you're in the garden every day.

For some of us, it can still be warm enough to sit outdoors comfortably, at least for a couple of hours. And many plants that are considered summer-flowering, such as dahlias, fuchsias, and roses, can look as good in the first half of fall as at any time of the year. The garden can also be at its most colourful with the warm tones of late-flowering heleniums and rudbeckias and the rich, golden-brown glows of miscanthus. Dahlias continue to dazzle, and a whole spectrum of different asters will burst onto the scene. Annual plants in pots can still be flowering their hearts out too and looking as full and colourful as in summer. And the intense colouration of tree and shrub leaves just before they drop is still weeks away.

The arrival of fall is something of a drawn-out process, but as the weeks progress, every gardener has an overarching feeling of something drawing to a close. Perhaps the garden is a bit like a footballer coming to the end of their career but still capable of wowing the crowds and teaching the young pretenders a thing or two every now and then. The fearless impetuousness of youth has gone but the bold, confident attributes of maturity are an able replacement.

Roses that shimmered brightly in the midsummer sun now glow in its low rays, with weaker but more complex shades. Subtle browns are creeping into the edges of flowerheads that only weeks ago were showing the sharpest of zingy colours. Fall is the most graceful season. Perennial plants become more complex as they slowly fade, eventually leaving a monochrome skeleton, a plant that is there but not there.

Fall is also a season of harvest, a season that offers tangible rewards on top of all the others already mentioned. Besides providing crops to gather and store, it beckons us with tender plants that can grow year after year but that will most likely perish if left in the garden.

And as fall progresses, it inevitably becomes a season of reflection. Allthough eventually emptied of many things that had just recently given it its fullness, the garden keeps on giving as the season changes character and our plants evolve and age. As 30-minutes-a-day gardeners we can reflect on what's gone and (ideally anyway) gain a deeper sense of what it means to appreciate things when we have them. The beauty of this in the garden is that no plant is gone forever. The cycle of sowing, planting, and propagating gives us endless new chances to restore what once was. Perennial plants teach us lessons about regeneration as they die down to straw-like material or mushy leaves, only to rise majestically again. With this in mind, we can see fall as a season of hope, so long as we trust that spring will come and that the place is still beautiful while we wait.

1

Colourful
plants for fall

———

Flowering shrubs and hardy annuals will bring vivid colours to the garden in fall. Berries can be a bonus.

1. Hardy fuchsias

These reliable shrubs make great garden features as they get larger, with hundreds of pendulous blooms dripping from arching stems in an avalanche of pinks, reds, and purples. They can be pruned back to 10cm (4in) above ground level in early spring if they've grown too big for their space, and they can be trimmed to shape through the growing season to contain their vigorous, but never unmanageable, growth. The berries are edible too, if you fancy an extra fall crop from the garden.

2. New England asters

These hardy, bushy perennials will sit in the garden almost unnoticed through summer, but that's no bad thing. They will let summer-flowering plants take centre stage without muscling in, then almost behind your back will slowly build up into a bushy perennial covered in buds by the time fall arrives. Then in the second half of fall until winter takes over, these asters show off sprays of small but pretty flowers in a range of cool pink and purple pastel shades.

3. Marguerites

These free-flowering plants are like osteospermums in terms of what they need in order to survive winter, but they will still make great annual plants even if they succumb. They cover themselves with white, orange-centred, daisy-like flowers and if fed with a half-strength high-potassium liquid plant food a few times through summer, they will flower and flower. Seeing these domes smothered with bright daisy flowers in fall is a real tonic.

2

3

4

4. Osteospermums

Also known as Cape daisies, these tender perennial plants usually succumb to winter wet and freezing temperatures, although they may survive in a pot filled with well-draining compost set in a sheltered spot close to a house wall. That aside, they are worth growing even if winter finishes them off, because they start flowering in midsummer in all sorts of shades from cool whites to deepest orange and continue all the way through until winter. Place in a sunny spot on the patio and water well in dry spells. Keep deadheading for months of cheerful flowers.

A season of discovery

Learning to love the garden, however it is

The garden at the start of fall is likely to be as crammed as at any other point in the year. This is probably the time when you will realize what sort of look you really want it to have. Whether you want it to be a higgledy-piggledy place with no room for manoeuvre, a bit like a house stuffed to the rafters with ornaments and seemingly unnecessary furniture, or whether a place with some deliberately open spaces and order is more to your taste. There is, of course, no right or wrong way and sometimes you don't know what you want until you experience something that you know you don't. When I had a tiny, courtyard city-centre garden, less than 10m (30ft) long and around 2.5m (8ft) wide, I realized in the second fall that I found the place too full. I had been slowly planting up more and more containers and letting plants get bigger and bigger, and I felt that the garden didn't have a focus anymore. It had become a mass of green.

Fall is a good time to decide what you want more or less of, because once summer is over, the most-used parts of the garden, the most appreciated plants, and the demands on the space to suit your lifestyle have all become more evident. With the majority of your plants as prominent now as at any other point in the year, you may also realize that you want to replace some areas of planting with a feature instead. Maybe more seating, a storage space, or a quirky sculpture or wooden planter.

The look of a garden is always in a state of transition, especially when it contains vegetable crops.

Opposite: Fall is the time when some plants run out of steam and are cleared away.

Whatever you decide you need to do (which could be nothing), I like to embrace fall regardless, rather than look at the garden and shake my head. The wonder of how much some plants have managed to grow is easily lost if you simply use the season as an excuse to feel bad about the place, or yourself. I much prefer to see gardening as a continual process of trial and error, with the "errors" still an opportunity for something positive. Maybe a plant that has ended up being too big can go to a friend with a bigger garden or can be cut back and moved into a pot to keep it in check. Perhaps you've discovered something that you wished you had planted more of. That one is easily solved for next year.

Getting rich slow

Investing in fall

It took Warren Buffett decades to become a billionaire. When Amazon founder Jeff Bezos asked him, "Why doesn't everyone just copy you?" Buffett famously replied, "Because nobody wants to get rich slow," or so the story goes.

Whether it is apocryphal or not, can there possibly be a lesson here for gardeners? Most definitely! There's a reason why beautiful displays of fall-planted bulbs go viral on Instagram in spring. In an instant-gratification, short-term, dopamine fix–dependent culture, taking the time to do something outdoors in the cold that will give results in five or six months' time is going against the grain and about as current as Noah building his ark.

Pottering around in the garden might also be a galaxy away from the world of multimillion-dollar deals, but it can mirror the rewards to be found in patient, long-term investing. In fact, a few simple steps in fall will pay off with some big results the next spring, summer, and beyond. So much so that you may well ask yourself, "Why doesn't everybody just copy me?" Ok, so you don't have millions of dollars to show for it—at least you're spared having to deal with hangers-on and long-lost relatives coming out of the woodwork—but you will have a richer, more colourful garden.

The most obvious long-term investment in fall is in planting bulbs. It's a traditional fall job that you will never regret doing come spring. You might forget that you did it though. It's one of those tasks that will come perfectly naturally to you if you are an uber-organized planner. If you're more of a last-minute doer, then set a reminder (or three or four) on your phone or calendar. Yes of course you can plant potted bulbs in spring and find forced plants in nurseries or plant centres. But you will have to go to great expense to create anything as beautiful and natural looking as drifts of fall-planted bulbs.

You'll know you're a 30-minutes-a-day gardener when you take the time to pause at the garden a moment to remember that it is giving us a tremendous opportunity to get rich slow, a richness that can't be taken away by financial crashes, scammers, or our human weakness to always want more. The feelings of hope, joy, and new life as bulbs planted in fall burst open in spring are something deeper, and it's yours time after time. Even in the dystopian springs of 2020 and 2021, the bulbs burst brightly—nothing could take that away.

Planting spring-flowering bulbs

There isn't much science to planting spring bulbs. The key thing is just to remember—and find time—to do it. The act of planting when so many plants are fading before our eyes is actually quite a difficult thing to prioritize doing. Spring seems a lifetime away and there are also some practical considerations, the main one being finding space to plant your bulbs. The garden and patio can be at their fullest in fall, especially if you leave perennials intact to enjoy their structure over winter and to give the birds something to nibble on.

There are some good bulb-planting principles to follow, though:

- As a rule of thumb, plant bulbs at a depth equal to twice the height of one bulb.

- Before planting bulbs on clay soils, mix a handful of grit into planting holes and mix it together with the soil to help drainage. If you leave a pile of grit unmixed at the bottom, it will act like a sump, and winter wet can cause the bulbs to rot.

- Plant tulips late, at the end of fall. They grow fast and hate being cold and wet. The less time they are in the soil before it warms up, the better they will grow.

- Cram bulbs close together in pots, as close as you can without letting them touch. Sparse displays of bulbs in pots look mean and gappy.

- Throw bulbs on the ground and plant them where they land if you're planting bulbs in grass and want a natural look.

- Only plant firm, clean, large bulbs that have no softness or green, rotten patches on them. You get what you pay for with bulbs. First-rate bulbs from a specialist are a sound investment.

Cram spring-flowering bulbs into pots in fall to create full and color-packed displays when the blooming season arrives.

To tidy or not to tidy?

Deciding what state to leave the garden in for winter

This may sound trite but gardeners usually fall into two camps: the tidy and the untidy. And you'll know which you are. If you seriously think of a leaf blower as a sound investment then you're highly unlikely to fall into the untidy category. And if your shed has all the tools *somewhere*, then you surely are. And I think this may translate into the type of fall gardener that you are too.

As fall sets in, no matter what we do, perennial plants start to look scruffy, trees start to shed leaves, border edges develop an overgrown fringe, and the abiding feeling in the garden is one of a party that is coming to an end before the next one starts. If you've got space or are clever with the use of plants in containers in a small area, the party can start again as winter bites. Evergreen conifers can take centre stage for their colour and form, shrubs with brightly colored stems look great, and winter-flowering shrubs such as viburnum and witch hazel will arrive later to add sweet scent and delicate blossom.

But there is no doubt that, on the face of it, the garden in fall will look like it needs a good tidy up. Does it though? Well the easy answer is that it definitely doesn't in order for the place to regenerate in spring. Dormant plants will re-emerge in their own time. Unpruned plants will continue to grow when conditions are right, regardless of whether they were pruned or not. And leaving plants intact is helping to provide suitable environments for mammals to hibernate and food for

Fallen leaves provide a natural mulch for newly planted hedges, helping to suppress weeds.

Opposite: Summer-cropping vegetables that are no longer productive, such as peas, are best removed and composted.

Making leafmould

Perhaps the most beautiful thing about the gorgeous, slowly but beautifully dying fall leaves is that when their outstanding colours finally fade away, they leave a legacy for future generations. What am I talking about? I'm referring to the contribution to the garden that these old leaves make if we collect them into heaps or bag them and let them decompose. Eighteen months later (remember "get rich slow"?) you'll have a beautiful, crumbly substance that is as rich and useful as the most premium bagged compost in the garden store.

Although this is usually considered an fall task, it's also good for keeping warm if you want to do some gardening in winter. I have two narrow boxwood hedges in my front garden that sit near an old sycamore tree. In fall the fallen leaves cover the ground around the hedge, making a handy mulch that stops weeds growing here while the weather is still mild. So I let them do their thing to protect the hedge before gathering them up at the end of the year, already on their way to breaking down.

birds and insects. There will come a point when it's time to clear away old growth and compost it to make way for the new. But it doesn't have to be in fall.

However, some perennials don't look good in fall and winter, particularly those without attractive seedheads, so you'll probably want to fast-track them to the top of the compost heap. Old climbing annuals such as sweet peas, morning glories, or black-eyed Susans can also be a bit of an eyesore as they fade and decay, so they may be best removed. There is no right or wrong, but whatever you do, don't be hard on yourself if the garden looks a mess as fall progresses. It's a natural process, like shedding skin or losing touch with the younger generation.

In fall, however, it's also worth bearing in mind that gardens will always be artificial spaces, unless they are truly left as a complete wilderness. So some plants will need a helping hand through the year and sometimes it pays to do it in fall. Perennial plants that are not guaranteed to survive the winter in your garden will appreciate your timely intervention. Removing old, wet, decaying plant material that dies down at the base of a plant and replacing it with a thick dry mulch of composted bark or bark chippings will help insulate any exposed part of the plant against severe cold and winter wet. Other potential survivors might need lifting from the ground completely to help them make it through winter. Which we will get to next.

The salvage operation

Gathering the last crops of the year

Harvesting is a part of being a gardener that conjures up a whole host of emotions. Maybe for you it's purely the satisfaction of offering an end product on the mealtime table for the family to eat or for your desktop work-from-home lunch. But it could be more. It's easy to disconnect from the process involved in growing a crop—let's say beetroot—from seed sitting in a packet in the kitchen cupboard at the end of winter to the hefty tennis ball–sized root prized from the soil in fall if you just sow the seeds and forget about them. Not so easy when being out in the garden every day is a way of life.

After you've observed and coaxed your crops through the growing season, the final harvest can be poignant for long-term crops. As you pull them from the soil for the final time, perhaps it reminds you of all that's happened in your life in the months since you planted them out. And whatever you went through, the crop itself was a constant. Maybe it was something to look after to take your mind off things, a focal point for teaching children, or a talking point for when your friends came to visit. So harvesting is a time to celebrate but

Keep those babies dry

When conditions start to get a bit damp in fall, pop some old carpet or weed-suppressing fabric underneath winter squashes that are still developing to keep wet earth from causing them to rot. Harvest them before the first frost arrives.

also perhaps a moment of reflection, a moment to be thankful for the year that—in terms of growing—is about to pass.

As well as gathering edible crops, now—before the first frost of the season—is also a time to gather plants that are exotic visitors to your climate to keep them indoors over winter. This could be as simple a process as moving a potted plant onto a well-lit porch or it could be lifting dahlia tubers (the bulky bits under the ground) and keeping them in a tray of sand in the garage. You can actually wait until the first frost blackens the foliage, then lift them, so don't panic if you think they have been killed. There is a great feeling of satisfaction when those first glimmers of new growth reappear at the end of winter, and the plants can be watered and potted up to get them growing strongly again. Be sure to do the salvage operation early enough to make sure that plants aren't exposed to any temperatures that could harm them.

If you have permanently planted trees, shrubs, or perennials in the garden that aren't hardy enough to survive the winter, now is the time to protect them. Plants with trunks such as bananas or palms can be protected by putting a ring of chicken wire around the plant and stuffing it with straw. Add an additional covering of fleece to provide extra protection.

Onions planted in spring need harvesting before the weather turns cold and wintry.

What to harvest in fall

There is a lot to harvest in fall but also a lot of crops that are hardy enough to be kept in the ground through winter, such as beetroot, parsnips, and carrots, especially if your soil in the garden or compost mix in pots is free draining. However, as mornings turn damp and misty and night-time temperatures drop, some veggies will need gathering up quickly before winter arrives:

Summer squashes

This diverse group of colourful fruits of all shapes and sizes needs harvesting before frost turns them to a gooey mush. These are commonly called courgettes and marrows, while some are simply known as summer squash. The key difference between summer and winter types is that the summer types won't form a rock-hard skin that protects the flesh inside. Deciding exactly when to harvest summer squash can be a bit like a game of Dare: how long do you dare leave it? Cold nights can cause young, developing fruits to rot. Remember that you can freeze these crops to add to stews and soups so even if you have too many to eat and want to leave them, you can play it safe and harvest to freeze for winter.

Chillies

If you've got some containers of chilli bushes showing off a promising array of still-developing fruits as summer turns to fall, consider moving the pots to a well-lit windowsill indoors to help the fruits ripen, if you can afford the windowsill space. It can be the difference between green and red fruits, if you are growing them primarily for the heat. I've experimented with treating chillies as houseplants and keeping them indoors all winter to bring outside again in spring. It can be done but you'll need a very well-lit room that follows the natural light as much as possible and that doesn't get any colder than 15°C (60°F). The plants will look scruffy in their first winter, but the old, woody trunks can look impressive in their second year, appearing almost like bonsai.

Beans

Climbing beans are warm-weather plants that are most at home in a tropical climate, and the transition from summer to fall is not to their liking. In my garden, I know it is time to say farewell when they start to get bashed about by the strong winds that signal that fall has well and truly arrived. The good news is that runner and French beans are good keepers and freezers, whether you are harvesting the whole pods or the jewel-like beans that are hidden inside. Runner beans can be sliced and frozen. Let haricot or borlotti bean pods dry on the plant; if you harvest them and the beans inside are firm, they will store indoors for up to a year in an airtight container—where they make an impressive kitchen feature if you keep them in something see-through.

AND DON'T FORGET

Onions

Onions planted as sets in spring need to be harvested in fall or they will go soft and mushy. Leave the necks intact and harvested onions can keep in a cool, dry place indoors right through winter. Any that are a bit soft when you dig them up should be used in the kitchen first. In fall, plant overwintering onion bulbs to harvest in spring.

Potatoes

Harvest your potatoes in early fall. It's tempting to leave them for as long as possible to get as big a crop as you can, but it's not worth the risk of wetness spoiling the tubers, and once foliage has died back, it's time to dig them up. Harvest on a dry, mild day and ideally leave the tubers on the soil surface to naturally dry out, then rub the dry soil off them and store them in paper bags with the top covered, in an unheated but frost-free place indoors. They can last all winter.

Tomatoes

The time to give up on your tomatoes is when the fruits stop ripening. Yes, you can harvest green fruits and make chutney but how many you want to harvest should really depend on how much you want chutney in your life. Fruits that are starting to "turn" can be brought indoors and placed near some bananas, which will release ethylene and help them ripen.

The joy of evergreens —yes really!

How "boring" plants lift the coming darkness

Fall is a good time for planting but it's easy not to have planting at the forefront of our minds at this time of year. Maybe you are preoccupied with deadheading, harvesting, or weeding, which can be full-on tasks in the fall garden. It's of course not the only time to plant and there may not be enough hours in the day, but planting evergreens is a rewarding thing to do, especially with winter around the corner. All of a sudden there comes a point when it is obvious that fall has, if you'll pardon the pun, fallen. Summer colour has gone, some plants have been cleared, there are gaps where crops once were, and the garden is becoming emptier by the day. What remains is what you will look out on for the cold season ahead.

Now there can be some fine highlights in winter: multi-coloured cornus (dogwood) with their warm, bright, bare stems. Cheerful snowdrops or crocuses as winter enters its later stages. Fragrant winter shrubs such as daphne and winter jasmine. But for me, a garden with good structure in winter feels a more inviting place than one that is mainly a flat, empty space. And fall is a good time to add more evergreen structure to the garden to give a feeling of fullness and

Fatsia japonica provides glossy, exotic-looking foliage in a sheltered corner to lift dark days.

Previous: Harvest potatoes in dry conditions and leave the tubers to dry before storing them indoors.

to provide some eye-catching focal points, including plants for the frost to beautify.

In early fall, the soil is still warm and hopefully not overly wet, and it is easier to see potential gaps now than in summer. Stand indoors looking out on the garden and think about what you would be able to see in winter once the summer flowers have gone. Ask a friend to go outdoors and stand where you would like to have extra points to focus on in winter. Push a cane in and you've identified a good home for a new evergreen. Maybe you'll end up putting a statue or a bird bath there instead. It doesn't matter what, but if it will help you feel like the garden is still an active space in winter, then so much the better.

Also look along the edges of paths and think about what they will look like in a few months' time. Maybe a zingy lime-green leaved *Carex oshimensis* 'Everillo' or a damp-loving lookalike *Acorus* 'Ogon' (or better still, three planted at intervals) would liven your winter walk to put out the trash or head off to work. It will lift the spirits and help to keep the connection with the garden strong in winter, when even the most experienced gardener can feel disengaged from the place, especially if the weather makes going out in the garden more difficult.

Evergreen sempervivums add detail and character to the edges of containers all year round.

MORE THINGS YOU CAN DO IN
THE GARDEN IN FALL

Trim back Mediterranean herbs.
Fall is a good time to trim evergreen Mediterranean herbs such as rose-
mary and lavender. Trim back every stem, making sure not to cut into woody
growth which is unlikely to reshoot well. Cut off more on the lower stems than
at the top. This will give them an attractive curved edge that will add some
stylish lines to the garden in winter. Pruning in winter can potentially damage
the plant, so it's best to tackle this now.

Mow a meadow.
If there's an area of grass that you've left to grow wild in the garden in order
to develop wildflowers and encourage pollinators, fall is a good time to cut it
back to about 8cm (3in) from ground level to help prevent grass from taking
over the meadow completely. Lay the cut material over walkways that get
muddy in winter or gradually add it to the compost heap in stages.

Take cuttings of shrubby plants.
As bare stems start to make themselves obvious in late fall, it's a reminder that
this is a good time to take hardwood cuttings. This might sound complicated
but it's an easy way to make more of your favourite shrubs. Take cuttings of
pencil-thick stems, around 30cm (12in) in length. Make a horizontal cut at the
bottom of the cutting, just below where a pair of leaves was. Use sharp secateurs. Make a sloping cut at the top, just above where a pair of leaves was.
Push the cuttings into deep pots that have been filled with compost and

Take 30cm-long (12in)
cuttings of shrubs
such as cornus, rubus,
and salix to make
more plants for free.

firm well. Water once, label the pot, then keep the cuttings in a sheltered corner outdoors. They should be ready to plant out in the following fall. Gently tip the pot upside-down and give it a gentle shake to check if the cuttings are rooted.

Plants to take hardwood cuttings from:

- buddlejas
- cornus
- currants
- forsythia
- gooseberries
- ribes
- willows

Plant evergreens.

Plant coniferous or broadleaf evergreens when the ground underfoot is moist but not waterlogged. Place at the same depth as the plant was in its pot, and firm the surrounding soil. Water well, then cover with a 5cm (2in) layer of mulch such as well-rotted garden compost, bark chippings, or gravel. If your soil is poor, mix a spadeful of well-rotted garden compost or bagged soil-based compost into the soil that you dug out for the planting hole before using the mixture to finish planting. If you are planting tall evergreens, secure the main stem to a stake to keep it upright. Remove the stake in the following summer when the plant should have established itself. Evergreen plants have a habit of not letting you know that they needed watering until after the event, when leaves turn brown at the ends or drop and it doesn't seem obvious why. Check them through fall and winter and if the soil is very dry, give them a soak, so long as the soil isn't frozen. Also check your evergreen plants in containers because strong winds can easily dry out the compost even if the air temperature is not very high and it seems an unlikely time to be watering plants.

Divide early-flowering perennials.

Fall is a good time to lift and split perennials that flower very early in spring and haven't been split for two or three years. This involves digging them up, splitting them into multiple, smaller plants, and then replanting them. This way they aren't disturbed when the plants are about to come into flower. Splitting the plants keeps them fresh and healthy and gives you new plants for free. Carefully prize the clumps up using a digging fork or a hand fork if the clump is small. Separate each one into new plants and replant them immediately into weed-free ground. Water after planting and during dry spells. Place a cane into the ground where you've planted the new divisions to remind you where they are when the leaves die back in winter.

Start some bulbous crops.

Don't forget that garlic and overwintering onions can be planted in fall in ground that isn't waterlogged. Overwintering onions are little bulbs that can be planted into well-drained soil and left to stay in the ground over winter to give you a crop of tasty salad onions in the following spring, or an early crop of large onions in late summer. Mix some grit or garden sand into the soil before planting to improve drainage. Garlic needs a prolonged cold period in order to produce the best crop. Planting in fall rather than the end of winter gives it every chance of experiencing a good cold snap.

8

So where do we go from here?

Stepping forward with confidence

The more things you try in the garden, the more exciting and adventurous a place it becomes.

It's a surprisingly mild evening in January but still cold enough for a fleece jacket and a coat. I'm sitting on a crumbling brick wall at the end of the garden, watching a bonfire crackle and glow. It's only six o'clock but it's been dark for two hours; in fact it never really got properly light all day. On the face of it, it doesn't seem like the ideal time to be a gardener. And it's not. The ground has been saturated for weeks, with no hope of planting or even weeding. So having a bonfire at this time has become a bit of a tradition. And I can lose myself for hours staring into the flames and embers, comforted by the soft crackles. Amid the gently, busy noise of burning logs it's another chance to "face north."

Being out in the garden, in the thick of it, a small pocket of ground warmed and lit by firewood feels as sweet as an hour sitting in the summer sun. Once the fire has died down, I head indoors but keep popping my head out of the back door to check that all is still under control. And then I see it, swathes of gangly stalks and flowerheads of *Verbena bonariensis* standing out like silhouettes, perfectly backlit by orangey flames and a billowing smoke. My garden, your garden, any garden, is the gift that keeps on giving. Come rain, shine, or winter cold, we just have to be looking for it.

So where do we go from here? Well, we've reached the end of this journey, but yours is only beginning. I hope that it has become clear that regardless of how long you have lived somewhere, if you've just gotten the 30-minute bug, you basically have a brand new garden. It's a bit like discovering a tv show that aired ten years ago, that has been loved by millions, but that you have only just started watching. It might be familiar to a lot of people. They might know a lot about it. But it's new to you. Or if you've been a keen gardener for a long time, then

A gardener's garden is never finished, and the paths of discovery are infinite and exciting.

I hope that you are able to unlock a way of *being* in the garden, knowing that the *doing* will then take care of itself.

This book is deliberately not a guide on how to grow everything. There are plenty of them out there, and some of my favourite references are listed at the back of this book. As you grow into the gardening way of life you will most likely start to devour some of these as you explore more of the wondrous things that can be added to the garden. That's my aim anyway. I hope that I have encouraged you to feel like you can grow everything and that this journey provides the platform for you to delve into new explorations. In fact, we could read a guide on how to grow every plant known to humanity, but if growing and gardening aren't a meaningful part of our lives, then it would likely be time wasted.

Gardening has long been a pastime that ebbs and flows in popularity, just like any other. My hope is that it ceases to be. That those who take it up don't pass it over after a few weeks like an unlearned musical instrument that's just sitting there gathering dust. The beauty of gardening is that there are always results to see, so long as we open our eyes to see them and tune ourselves to nature's frequency. And unlike that dust-covered guitar, it doesn't rely on our slavish service to enrich and enhance our lives.

Sometimes I speak to people who wouldn't identify themselves as gardeners but who tell me about everything that they want to have in their garden. And listening to their wish list, I feel like it's no wonder that they haven't embraced gardening very much. The gap between the reality of the garden now and the garden dreamed of is vast. Staring at it out of the window must just be a source of disappointment. Dipping your toe in the water and embracing the idea of spending time in the garden first and then "doing" second will shift the balance away from disappointment and into opportunity.

It doesn't matter if you don't have the garden that you want to have. Becoming a 30-minutes-a-day gardener is about how the garden can help you have the life you want (or didn't know that you wanted) to have.

And the more you try things out in the garden, the more that serendipitous things will happen. If you leave your garden intact at the end of summer to go to seed, then all manner of opportunistic seedlings can emerge, some exactly where you want them, some where you don't. But you get to be the editor and decide what stays. Leave a patch of self-sown seedlings to mingle with some of your other plantings or garden features and you'll most likely have a corner of the garden to be proud of, even though it wasn't the result of lots of hard graft, just some gentle coaxing and an open mind.

As the 30-minutes-a-day habit grows, so does the understanding that good things happen in the garden, even or especially when you don't insist on holding onto everything with a firm grip. Maybe some self-sown nasturtiums have found their way into a container and then proceeded to start scrambling through pots, using other plants as a ladder. This is not easily created by the gardener but allowed to happen naturally, and then it's easily enjoyed and easily controlled once nature has done its thing. Hold on to the belief that the garden is a place where good things happen, even if the whole place doesn't look how you would ideally like it to.

And above all else, don't worry about whether what you are doing in the garden is the right thing to do. The plants will soon tell you if they don't think so, but they tend to be more forgiving than those busy-body, self-appointed gardening experts that I seem to encounter more frequently than I would like to.

Of course, many of the tried and tested principles of gardening are there for a reason. Growing plants in conditions similar to those they encounter in the wild, staying off the garden when it is frozen or too wet, to name but two. Yet as you grow to love being in the garden and start to observe plants closely, you will more than likely discover that, at times, rules are there to be broken. Some plants will grow in a place where none of the growing advice suggests planting them. Others will randomly throw up a flower in a colour that they are not supposed to have. The more we delve into the world of the garden, the more we will have an open mind about it.

Why does this matter? I hope that this book conveys an essence of adventure. A belief that in your garden, anything could happen and wondrous things *do* happen on a daily basis. If we try to put plants, gardening tasks, and our growing conditions in a box, then we can turn gardening into a mechanical exercise that is hardly likely to inspire a generation to become 30-minutes-a-day gardeners.

Enjoy being in your garden on the dull days, the cold days, the blazing hot days, the depressed days, and the sunny, happy days. The days when you want to celebrate and the days when you want to mourn. The days when you harvest and the days when you sow. Whatever the weather or whatever is going on in your life, getting out there in the garden will keep you grounded.

The garden is a place where good things happen, like these nasturtiums scrambling through a pot.

Epilogue

I'm sitting in a city café in November and staring out of the window.

Before my eyes are enormous sheets of glass cladding the front of a shopping mall and rows and rows of regimented concrete slabs. At least the urban planners had the foresight to plant a semicircle of ginkgo trees around the outside of the café. December is less than a fortnight away, the leaves have all but lost their green pigment, and those being hit by the sunlight shine a glowing buttercup yellow.

The paving slabs are sprinkled with these leaves as if delicately strewn (but not smothered) with confetti from a wedding. I find this even more beautiful than the trees themselves. The tables and chairs outside the café—most of them empty except for a brave few souls who don't mind the fresh fall air—match the colours of nature's perfectly placed confetti. The finest painter, the fussiest film set designer, or the most meticulous window dresser could not position the leaves more precisely as they scatter the floor of the concrete jungle to remind anyone who wants to see it that the seasons are changing. Not because the mall has put up its tacky decorations but because these beautiful trees cannot hide their glory, even when they are shedding their skin for a winter of sleep.

The café is full of people easing into the day, some looking at laptops or chatting with friends, some with work folders, others with babies in prams, but I hope I'm not the only one taking in the subtle yet spectacular fall scene. It will have disappeared like a puff of smoke in two weeks, just like the finest spring blossom. I'm clutching my coffee, still staring, and if you've stayed with me to the end of this book, perhaps you will be there—still staring too.

Late fall leaves of *Ginkgo biloba* scatter like nature's confetti.

Further Reading

David Austin Roses. *2022 Handbook of Roses*. eu.david-austinroses.com/pages/handbook-2022.

Julia Cameron. 2016. *The Artist's Way: A Spiritual Path to Higher Creativity*, Anniversary Edition. New York, NY: TarcherPerigee.

Greg Loades. 2020. *The Modern Cottage Garden: A Fresh Approach to a Classic Style*. Portland, OR: Timber Press.

Tovah Martin. 2021. *The Garden in Every Sense and Season: A Year of Insights and Inspiration from My Garden*. Portland, OR: Timber Press.

James Rebanks. 2016. *The Shepherd's Life: Modern Dispatches from an Ancient Landscape*. New York, NY: Flatiron Books.

Geoff Stebbings. 2012. *Growing Your Own Fruit & Veg for Dummies*. Chichester, UK: John Wiley & Sons.

Acknowledgements

Thanks to everyone at Timber Press and Hachette Book Group who has made this book possible. To Tom Fischer, Andrew Beckman, and Mike Dempsey for believing in the idea and in me to write it. To Rebecca O'Malley for originally encouraging me to think about writing books. For this I will always be grateful. Special thanks to Eve Goodman for her amazing editing work and for encouraging me and steering the whole process so expertly.

Thanks to Neil Hepworth for photographing my garden so expertly while it was still very much in the early stages and backgrounds were tricky! Thanks for all the travelling and for finding the time to take photographs at such busy times of year. Thanks to Rob Cardillo for the inspiring images that capture so brilliantly the drama and celebration of the changing seasons. And to Julie Loder for letting me use her image that wonderfully encapsulates the essence of the book—that special things happen when we stop trying to tightly control every aspect of our gardens.

Thanks to David Austin Roses for the photo of 'Princess Anne' and for the beautiful roses in the garden that served as its focal point in the early stages and as a constant source of inspiration.

Thanks to my wonderful wife and kids for giving me the time to write this book amid the chaos of family life! Thank you God for blessing us with three beautiful boys.

Photography Credits

All photos by Neil Hepworth, except for the following:

David Austin Roses, page 53

BBA Photography / Shutterstock.com, page 163

keith burdett / Alamy Stock Photo, page 76

Rob Cardillo, pages 46, 74, 91, 93 (top left, top right, and middle left), 108, 118, 121, 126, 129, 132 (top left, top right, and bottom right), 134, 136, 152, 165, 166, 177, 182, 184, 185, 191, 208

christophe.dtr / Shutterstock.com, page 132

Peter Cripps / Dreamstime.com, page 88

GAP Photos, pages 59, 149

GAP Photos / Robert Mabic - Christina Shand, page 37; Nicola Stocken, page 93 (bottom left); Richard Bloom, page 93 (bottom right); Carole Drake, page 95; Elke Borkowski, page 104; BBC Magazines Ltd, page 141 (bottom left)

Bob Gibbons / Alamy Stock Photo, page 57

Greg Loades, pages 99 (bottom right), 192

Julie Loder, page 215

Wikimedia Commons / Photo ©2007 Derek Ramsey / Used under a GNU Free Documentation License, page 216

Index

Neil Hepworth

Greg Loades

is editor of *The Alpine Gardener* and writes frequently about gardens and gardening for magazines such as *Kew*, *LandScape*, and *Garden News*. His writing has also appeared in many popular publications, including *BBC Gardeners'* World magazine, where he was gardening editor, and the luxury garden publication *The English Garden*, where he was deputy editor. He served his apprenticeship in the rose industry in the UK. His first book, *The Modern Cottage Garden*, was published in 2020 to unanimously enthusiastic reviews.